The Ascent of Mount Sinai

Raniero Cantalamessa O.F.M. ... . Ascoli
Piceno, Italy, in July 1934. For eleven years he was
professor of the history of early Christianity and head
of the religious sciences department at the Catholic
University of the Sacred Heart, Milan. Since 1980, he
has held the appointment of preacher to the Papal
household. In this capacity, he delivers a meditation in
the presence of the Pope, cardinals, bishops and supe-
riors of religious orders every week during Advent and
Lent.

Fr Cantalamessa, who is a member of the Roman
Catholic delegation for dialogue with Pentecostal
Churches, has spoken at scores of international confer-
ences and given retreats for priests in England, Ireland,
Australia and USA. He is a prolific writer on spiritual
topics and has had more than a dozen books published
across the world.

The Ascent of Mount Sinai

A spiritual journey in search of the living God

RANIERO CANTALAMESSA

Translated by Alan Neame

Fount

An Imprint of HarperCollins*Publishers*

To John Paul II

witness to the Living God
in our day

Fount Paperbacks is an Imprint of
HarperCollins*Religious*
Part of HarperCollins*Publishers*
77–85 Fulham Palace Road, London W6 8JB

First published in Great Britain
in 1996 by Fount Paperbacks

1   3   5   7   9   10   8   6   4   2

A catalogue record for this book is
available from the British Library

ISBN 0 00 627947 3

Printed and bound in Great Britain by
Caledonian International Book Manufacturing Ltd, Glasgow, G64

Contents

PROLOGUE
Climb up to me

Dear reader, starting to read a new book is like setting out on a journey. It's only fair then, as you take up this one, that I tell you at the outset where this journey will be taking you and whither we shall be heading. We shall be heading for Mount Sinai in search of such signs as may speak to us about the Living God.

Before dawn when it's still pitch dark and the temperature is icy, pilgrims to the physical Mount Sinai set out from St Catherine's monastery, silently, singly or in little groups, and start climbing the innumerable steps to the peak, so as to be there in time to watch the sunrise, which is a most impressive sight.

We too shall be doing something of the sort. We shall be climbing our spiritual Sinai, so that from its heights we may contemplate the One of whom the sun is but a pale reflection; so that we too – if possible and in such ways as he may wish – may have our own small theophany, our personal manifestation of God. Our guides will be Moses, Elijah and, with them, many another veteran of Mount Sinai.

Sinai is a mysterious mountain, seeming to be everywhere

and nowhere in particular. Even its name is unstable; now Mount Horeb, now Mount Sinai. The one thing certain about it is that it's 'the mountain of God'. Such is the importance of what occurs on this mountain that, just as the Bible speaks of the 'God of Abraham', so it also speaks of the 'God of Sinai' (cf. Psalm 68:8; Judges 5:5). Whoever travels 'for forty days and forty nights', no matter where the journey has begun, always ends up on this mountain. Moses, while still a fugitive in Midian, one day 'led his flock to the far side of the desert and came to Horeb, the mountain of God' and there it was he received his vision of God in the burning bush and the revelation of God's name (cf. Exodus 3:1ff). So too Elijah, having walked for 'forty days and forty nights', reached the foot of this mountain (cf. 1 Kings 19:8).

And this is the mountain we too shall try to climb. But 'who shall climb the mountain of the Lord?' (Psalm 24:3); who would dare undertake such a journey? Scripture gives us the answer in one simple sentence: 'Moses climbed up to God and the Lord called to him from the mountain' (Exodus 19:3). Moses climbed and the Lord called him; he climbed because the Lord was calling him. Before any initiative on our part comes God's initiative. He it is who calls, he invites and, if you are reading these lines, it's a sign that he's calling you as well.

God's call: how subtle and yet how powerful it is! Animals feel the pull of the forest, man the pull of his woman, woman that of her man ... But infinitely deeper is the pull – though of a different order – that God exerts on the soul. 'You have made us for yourself, Lord, and our hearts are restless until they find peace in you.'[1]

'Climb up to me,' God says to Moses (Exodus 19:3; 24:12). Someone is calling us, waiting for us up there. We are doing the seeking since he has sought us first. We wouldn't be seeking him at all if we hadn't already found him. 'How can you seek what you haven't lost?' a holy monk used to say. 'You can only look for

God if you have already known him and then lost him.'² This is the situation of all of us, created to be the 'image of God'. Driven out of Paradise, no longer seeing the 'serene and gentle' countenance of his God, Adam still weeps in every human soul.

It won't take us long to discover the mountain we intend to climb isn't outside us but within us; so we can adopt the mystical poet's words as our own and say:

> I am a mountain in God, I must climb up me
> so that he may disclose his dear face to me.³

But Sinai is a rugged mountain too. Today's search for the Living God offers hardships and new obstacles never existing in the days of the Fathers or when St Bonaventure wrote *The Soul's Journey into God*. Most of these ancient itineraries would get cut short today or be totally impracticable for people who now are no longer accustomed to raising themselves through successive degrees of speculation but are only susceptible (at best) to proofs of historical and existential type. And ours is to scale the Sinai of today, not some idealized Sinai existing outside time; we want to encounter the God who is alive today, not merely know about the God who lived in the past. We want if possible to recover the sense of the Living God, the need for whom it is so acutely obvious in the world around us.

We shall try to do as the wise scribe does, who puts *nova et vetera*, new things and old, at the service of the Kingdom: that is, the voices of the Ancients and the voices of the Moderns. We are aware that the Living God is better known by experience than by argument, by 'contagion' rather than by discussion. So we shall not hesitate to have frequent recourse to famous soul-encounters with God, so that we can almost hear the living voice ring out from 'the great cloud of witnesses with which we are surrounded' (Hebrews 12:1).

We shall do our best to accept the invitation God extends to us from the pages of Scripture: 'Be still and acknowledge that I am God' (Psalm 46:10). 'Be still', that is to say, stop worrying, or even (as it was once translated) take a holiday (*vacate*) from everything and everybody, so that you can learn this one thing, worth more than life itself however: that I am God.

So let us seek our strength in God and resolve on the 'holy journey' in our hearts. In faith and humility let us say to him: 'Your face, Lord, I seek. Do not turn your face away from me' (Psalm 27:8–9).

1   Getting back to things

The Bible is dotted with texts that speak of God as the 'Living One'. 'He is the Living God,' says Jeremiah (Jeremiah 10:10). 'I am the Living One,' God himself tells Ezekiel (Ezekiel 33:11). In one of the loveliest psalms in the Psalter – one written during the Captivity – the psalmist exclaims: 'My soul thirsts for God, the Living God' (Psalm 42:2). And again: 'My heart and body cry out for joy to the Living God' (Psalm 84:2).

Here clearly we have a metaphor drawn from human experience. The Jews adopted it to distinguish their God from the idols which, it says in one of the psalms, 'have mouths but say nothing, have eyes but see nothing, have ears but hear nothing, and they have no breath in their mouths' (Psalm 135:16–17). In contrast to the idols, the God of the Bible is 'a God who breathes'. An image, this, which seems very acceptable when we reflect that the Holy Spirit is actually said to be the breath, the breathing (*Ruah*) of God.

After the long predominance of idealism and the triumph of the 'idea' in recent times, even secular thought has felt the need for a return to 'reality', expressing it in the catch-phrase: 'Back to things!'[4] That is to say: not to stop short at given formulations of reality, at the theories constructed about it, at what is commonly thought about it, but to focus directly on the reality itself lying at the base of all; to remove the various layers of soil that have accumulated, and discover the underlying rock.

We must apply this programme in the religious sphere too. Of faith it has been said that 'it does not have a proposition as its term, but a reality'.[5] And what does 'getting back to things' mean when it's a matter of the supreme 'thing' within the sphere of religion, I mean, God? Just that: it means getting back to the Living God; breaking through, as it were, the terrible wall of the idea we have made for ourselves about him, and running open-armed to meet him in person. Discovering that God is not an abstraction, but a reality.

We see all things by the reflected and diffused light of the sun, but rarely do we raise our eyes to gaze at the sun itself. We cannot bear it. So it is with the Living God: 'In him we live and move and exist' (Acts 17:28), yet rarely do we raise the eyes of the mind to him who is the source of all. Even for believers, God is often, as it were, left in the background.

The programme 'Getting back to things' has had a justly famous application, leading to the discovery that things . . . exist! This is what its inventor had to say about it:

> I was sitting in the public gardens. The root of the chestnut tree plunged into the ground, right under my bench. I no longer remembered it was a root. Words had disappeared and with them the meaning of things, the way they are used, the tenuous signs of recognition that human beings have traced on their surfaces. I was sitting, rather huddled up, with head bowed, alone, facing that black, knotty, totally ugly mass that made me feel afraid. And then I had this flash

of illumination. It took my breath away. Before these recent
days, of course, I had anticipated what 'to exist' means. I was
like other people, like the ones walking along by the sea in
their spring clothes. Like them, I said: 'The sea is green; that
white spot on it is a seagull,' but I did not feel that it existed,
that the seagull was a 'seagull-existing'; normally existence is
in hiding. It is there, around us, we cannot say two words
without talking about it, and yet we cannot touch it. When I
thought I was thinking about it, I was evidently thinking
about nothing, my head was empty or with only a word in it,
the word 'being'. And then, look, at a stroke, there it was, as
clear as day: existence was suddenly unveiled.[6]

The philosopher who made this 'discovery' was a self-proclaimed
atheist, therefore he didn't go beyond acknowledging that the self
exists, that the world exists, that things exist. We however for our
part can set out from this experience, making it – as is in the
nature of all created things (cf. Romans 1:20) – a springboard to
the discovery of another Existent, the spark making possible
another enlightenment. Why shouldn't what was possible with
the chestnut root be in fact possible with God? Is God perhaps
any less real to the human mind than the chestnut root to our
eyes? In the service of the faith, the Fathers never thought twice
about appropriating those intuitions of truth to be found in
pagan philosophers, even in those determinedly hostile to
Christianity. We should copy them and do the same in our own
day.

What then can we appropriate to our purpose from this
particular philosopher's 'flash of illumination'? No direct application – not of content – only an indirect one – of method; but this is
quite enough to justify our being grateful to its author. Read with
a certain mental disposition favoured by grace, his account seems
perfectly tailored to jolt us out of our routine, to arouse in us first

the suspicion, then the certainty, that a knowledge of God exists that is as yet unknown to us. That, perhaps, before this moment we have never sensed what it means to say that God 'exists', that he is an existing-God or, as the Bible has it, a Living-God. And that therefore we have a task before us, a discovery to be made: to discover that God 'is there', so that we too, for a second, may have our breath taken away. That would be the adventure of a lifetime.

The words best suited for describing this programme of ours are: becoming aware of God. 'Becoming aware' indicates a sudden opening of our eyes, a jolt of knowledge, as a result of which we begin to see something that was there already but we hadn't seen hitherto.

With that same 'illumination' still in mind, let us once again read the story of the burning bush, for the episode takes place on the very slopes of Sinai (cf. Exodus 3:1ff). This will serve, among other things, to show how modern 'existential' thought can also help us discover something new in the Bible, something that ancient thought, exclusively geared to the ontological approach, was for all its riches unable to detect.

The biblical passage that tells of the burning bush is itself a burning bush. It burns, but is not consumed. With the passing of thousands of years it has lost nothing of its power to convey the sense of the divine. Among other things, it shows, better than any lecture, what happens when someone actually does encounter the Living God. 'Moses thought: Let me go nearer . . .' Observe this: he thinks and wills. He is in command; he is the one to call (or believe he calls) the tune. But at this point the divine breaks in with its own being and imposes its own law. 'Moses, Moses! Come no nearer. I am the God of your ancestors.' Everything is instantly changed. At a stroke, Moses becomes meek and submissive. 'Here I am,' he answers and covers his face, as the Seraphim were to cover their eyes with their wings (cf. Isaiah 6:2). The 'numinous' is in the air. Moses enters into the mystery.

In this atmosphere, God reveals his name: 'I am he who is.' Transplanted into the soil of Hellenistic culture and as early as the Septuagint, the phrase in Exodus 3:14: 'I am he who is' was being interpreted as a definition of what God is, the absolute Being, as an affirmation of his deepest essence. But an interpretation of this sort, exegetes tell us today, 'is completely at odds with the thought-patterns of the Old Testament'. The phrase more properly means: 'I am he who is *here*', or more simply still: 'I am here (or: I shall be here) for you!'' Here we have a concrete, not an abstract, statement; it refers to God's existence rather than to his essence, more to his 'being here' than to 'what' he is. We are not far from the 'I live', 'I am the Living One' which God proclaims in other parts of the Bible.

So that day, Moses discovered something very simple, yet something able to set in motion and sustain all subsequent history. He discovered that the God of Abraham, Isaac and Jacob exists, is here, is a reality present and active in history, someone on whom one can rely. And this was exactly what Moses needed to know at that moment.

The philosopher's experience with the chestnut root and that of Moses with the burning bush have this in common. Both Sartre and Moses discover the mystery of existence; the former, the existence of things; the latter, the existence of God. But whereas discovering that God exists proves a source of courage and joy, just discovering that things exist produces, Sartre avows, only 'nausea'.

If by God's grace it should be granted us too to have, in some degree, an illumination and revelation similar to those we have attempted to describe thus far by recourse to philosophy and the Bible, it should not astonish us if we spend the rest of our lives repeating over to ourselves, after each failure and disappointment, before each temptation to lose heart, and at every problem: 'But God is here, and that's more than enough! God's here and that's more than enough!'

Now let us pray that what we say 'about' the Living God may also always be said 'to' the Living God, in his presence and not in his absence. With St Anselm of Canterbury, who more than anyone laboured to show that our God is an Existing-God, let us say:

> Teach me, Lord, to seek you,
>   and show yourself to me as I seek.
> I cannot seek you if you do not teach me,
>   nor find you if you do not show yourself to me.
> May I seek you in desiring you,
>   desire you in seeking you,
> find you in loving you
>   and love you in finding you.[8]

2   God, the feeling of a presence

But what does it mean? How can one define the Living God? For a short while I entertained the notion of answering this question by drawing a profile of the Living God from the Bible; later, I saw this would have been a very stupid thing to do. To try to describe the Living God, to draw his portrait, even though basing oneself on the Bible, is to fall back into the temptation of reducing the Living God to an *idea* of the Living God.

For the same reason, I have decided not to organize the contents of this book into sections and sub-sections; instead I have adopted a scheme of short chapters, following on from one another without a break, like so many steps to the peak of our Sinai. This being so, what binds the whole thing together will not be so much a 'logic' as a 'reality', he himself, the Living God. He it will be who determines the arrangement of all the thoughts and ideas in it, just as a magnet organizes the iron filings that fall within its field of force.

The Living God, in as much as he is living, can be vaguely intuited by us; we can have a kind of feeling or presentiment about him. This may arouse desire or yearning for him. Nothing more. Life cannot be contained within an idea. In God 'to live and to intend are the same thing'⁹ and this suffices to show that, at the apex of all, there is no opposition *per se* between idea and reality, between life and thought, and hence between the Living God and the idea of him. But this is so only in God, not in us; when it is God who makes an idea of himself, not when we set about making an idea of God for ourselves. In the first case, idea and life stand on the same level; in the second, there is an infinite gap between the two.

Hence the sense or feeling of him is more rewarding than the idea, for the idea circumscribes the person, whereas the feeling reveals his presence while leaving it in its entirety and indeterminacy. This is why St Gregory of Nyssa speaks of the highest form of knowledge of God as a 'feeling of presence'.[10]

Rather than feeling, perhaps in this connection we should be using the terms 'perception' or 'intuition'. At any rate the feeling of which we are speaking has nothing whatever to do with the romantic or religiose acceptation of the word. We could even call it a quality of idea, such as we find in certain thinkers who have had a 'passion' for thought, thought therefore in which all life, its existential aspects too, is involved.

Even someone who has had the most extraordinary mystical perception of God is in fact like someone who has had a very vivid dream and who, on waking up, retains a clear 'impression' of what he saw in the dream without however being able to recall, try as he may, how the dream unfolded and what its contents were; yet nonetheless continues to feel the sweetness born of it distilling in his heart.[11]

The phenomenology of religion shows that the divine is in a category altogether different from any other, that it cannot be defined but only hinted at.

There is only one way to help another to an understanding of it. He must be guided and led on by consideration and discussion of the matter until he reaches the point at which the 'numinous' in him perforce begins to stir, to start into life and into consciousness. We can cooperate in this process by bringing before his notice all that can be found in other regions of the mind, already known and familiar, to resemble, or again to afford some special contrast to, the particular experience we wish to elucidate.[12]

There where no resemblance is possible, the opposite and the contrasting, rather than analogy, often prove to be the best way to knowledge. So here too that principle applies according to which 'God is pleased to reveal himself by his opposite' (*sub contraria specie*).

The Bible itself always speaks of God in apophatic, that is to say, negative or allusive terms: 'What no eye has seen and no ear has heard, what the human mind cannot visualize . . .'; or by questions: 'To whom can you compare me?', 'Who has ever been his counsellor?', 'O man, who are you to dispute with God?'; or by exclamations: 'Holy, holy, holy!', 'The Lord, the Lord, God of tenderness and compassion!', 'How rich and deep are the wisdom and knowledge of God!'; or, finally, yet more often by imagery and symbol: God is light, life, living water, fire, rock.

What we too can do as we think about the Living God is to go beyond 'the tenuous signs of recognition that human beings have scratched on his surface', and break the little shells containing our ideas about God, or the 'alabaster pots' in which we confine him, so that his fragrance may spread abroad and 'fill the house'.

St Augustine is a master at doing this. In a sermon to his people (not therefore in a tract written for the learned), he comes out with this exclamation: 'Shatter the idols within your own hearts!' The idols he is talking about are not external ones of wood or marble, but the ones inside. Not the idols of the pagans but the idols of the Christians. Someone, he says, pictures God the Creator as a great blacksmith who makes, arranges, fits together, polishes, turns things about: that's an idol of God! Someone else imagines him as a great monarch seated on a throne: that's an idol of God![13]

St Augustine has also bequeathed us what we might call a method for elevating ourselves in heart and mind to the true and Living God. It consists in repeating to ourselves each time after thinking about God: 'But God isn't this, this isn't God!' Think about the earth, think about the heavens, think about the angels or about anything or anyone whatever; lastly think about what you yourself think about God, each time repeating: 'Yes, but this isn't God, God isn't this!' 'Look beyond us,' one by one, all the created things we ask reply.[14] We must believe in a God beyond the God in whom we believe!

There is a unique quality about the Living God: he is the Entire, whereas the various representations of God are not the Entire, but only a part, a fragment. At the height of the Middle Ages with all their subtle distinctions about God (nature and persons, essence and existence, attributes, perfections and so on) introduced by scholastic theology with its method of the '*distinguo*', there was a contemplative who perceived what an obstacle all this created for the soul in search of God in his totality and simplicity, and who gave vent to a cry which we may sum up as this: 'God, be mine entire!'[15]

This notwithstanding, we can't help asking ourselves one question. Whom are we addressing when we utter the word 'God' without further specification? When in the Old Testament the psalmist says: 'O God, you are my God' (Psalm 63:1), to whom does this 'you' refer? Who was, so to speak, answering on the other end of the line? This 'you' is not just God the Father, the first Person of the Trinity, for how could the first Person have existed or be imagined for a single moment without the other two? No, nor is it the indeterminate Divine Essence, as though a divine essence were to exist which only at some later stage would crystallize out into God the Father, Son and Holy Spirit.

The one God, he who in the Bible says: 'I am', is the Father who begets the Son and with him (or through him) breathes the Spirit, sharing his entire divine nature with them. He is the God of loving fellowship, in whom *unity* and *trinity* proceed from the same root and from the same act to form a *Tri-unity*, in which neither of the two qualities – unity and plurality – precedes the other or exists without the other, in which neither of the two levels is above the other or 'deeper' than the other.

This is the Entire which we need and with which we are trying to enter into fellowship. The Living God of the Christians, in a word, is no other than the Living Trinity. The doctrine of the Trinity is contained *in nuce* in the revelation of God as love. To say: 'God is love' (1 John 4:8) is to say: God is a Trinity. St Augustine explains the matter thus: every love implies a lover, a beloved and a love uniting them. But we too can explain the matter for ourselves, if in a slightly different way. God is love. But we know that every love is a love of someone or something; there is no such thing as a love *in vacuo*, without an object. Now, whom does God love, for him to be defined as love? Human beings? But then, this love only dates back some hundred million years. The universe? But then, this love only dates back a few tens of billions. What about before then? Whom did God love, for him to be love?

By conceiving of God primarily as 'thought', the Greek thinkers and, generally speaking, religious philosophies of every age have given as their reply: God thought himself; he was 'pure' thought. But this is no longer acceptable once we say God is primarily 'love', since 'pure love of himself' would be pure egoism, which is not the raising of love to the highest degree but the total negation of it. And here is revelation's answer, as made explicit by the Church: God is love from the beginning, *ab aeterno*, for, even before there existed any object outside himself for him to love, he had within him the Word, the Son, whom he loved with infinite love, that is to say, 'in the Holy Spirit'.

This doesn't explain 'how' the unity can simultaneously be trinity (for us, an impenetrable mystery since occurring only in God), but it is enough at least for us to intuit 'why', in God, unity has also to be plurality, has also to be trinity. It is *because* 'God is love'! A God who was pure Knowledge, or pure Law, or pure Power, would certainly not need to be threefold (for this would enormously complicate matters); but a God who is love above all, yes, he would, since 'between less than two, love cannot be'. 'The world must know', writes De Lubac, 'that the revelation of God as Love confounds all it had previously conceived about the Godhead.'[16] So Christians believe in only one God, who is nonetheless no *solitary* God.

With St Augustine who has kept us company during this meditation, let us pray:

> O Lord my God, my only hope, hear me
> and let me never be too tired to go on searching for you
> but evermore with ardour seek your face . . .
> Before you, stand my strength and my weakness:
> preserve the one, heal the other.
> May I remember you,
> understand you
> and love you.[17]

3 When I seek you, I seek happiness

Let us take a step forward in our attempt, if not to 'define' him, at least to open some chink on to the reality of the Living God. We have already said: God is love; we ought forthwith to add: God is happiness! He is 'the joyful God who makes human beings joyful', says St Augustine.[18] Being happy and making others happy are as natural to him as shining and endowing things with colour are to light. Happiness is part of the very mystery of his being. Being Supreme Good, he is also supreme and infinite happiness. 'You are joy and gladness', St Francis exclaims in his *Page of Praises for Brother Leo*. To the catechist's question: 'Who is God?' it would be very right to teach a child to reply: 'God is the *happiest* being, creator of heaven and earth.' It would be no less accurate than saying 'most perfect', and would certainly be easier for the child to understand, for it would instantly and rightly associate happiness with play.

But how do we know that God is happiness? God is happiness for exactly the same reason as he is trinity: because he is love. Happiness after all – and we know this from experience – lies in loving and being loved. Agreed, truth too and knowledge make us happy, but only if this is accompanied by love. Now, from eternity, God with infinite love loves the Son, who with an equally infinite love loves him in return. In him, the Father finds 'all his delight', his happiness, that is to say. 'This ineffable embrace of the Father and his Image', says Augustine,

> is not therefore without pleasure, without love or without joy, and this love, this delight, this happiness within the Trinity is the Holy Spirit, who was not begotten, but is the sweetness of the begetter and the begotten pouring out upon all creatures according to their capacity.[19]

The Holy Spirit, by pouring the love of God into our hearts (cf. Romans 5:5), at the same time pours God's happiness into them as well, for the one is inseparable from the other. This is why one of the first fruits of his coming into the soul is joy (cf. Galatians 5:22). For, given that love tends of its nature to spread abroad, behold how God 'has created all things to fill his creatures with every blessing and lead all men to the joyful vision of his glory'.[20] God's happiness is like an overflowing river which, with its streams, 'makes glad the city of God', which is the world entire. 'The God of my joy and gladness' (more literally, 'joy of my gladness') is what one of the psalmists calls God (Psalm 43:4).

Since God is happiness, everything he does he does with joy: he creates with joy, 'to the joyful concert of the morning stars and unanimous acclaim of the sons of God' (Job 38:7), he saves with joy, he even suffers with joy (for it is also true that God 'suffers' with and for human beings, so long as our capacity for self-destruction endures). 'And I saw', Dame Julian of Norwich tells us, 'that God rejoices: rejoices that he is our father, rejoices that he is our mother, rejoices that he is our true spouse and that our soul is his beloved wife.'[21] God rejoices! A new, unstereotyped statement about God, apter than any treatise in making us feel him as a 'Living' God.

All this tells us something essential about the goal we have set for our journey: the road to the Living God is also the road to happiness. 'When I look for you to be my God, I am looking for happiness', to quote Augustine once more.[22] The mountain which we have decided to climb is the same one as all human beings are bent on scaling. Most times, up the wrong side, unfortunately. Everyone wants to be happy. At the sound of the word happiness, people prick up their ears, so to speak, and look to see if perhaps you have something on offer to quench their thirst. It is the one thing everyone has in common, without exception, be they good or bad. No one indeed would be bad if they didn't hope to become happy this way. If we could make a mental picture for ourselves of the whole human race at its deepest motivation, we should see an immense crowd gathered round a fruit tree, standing on tiptoe, desperately reaching out their hands in an attempt to pluck fruit which for ever eludes their grasp. Happiness, Dante says, is

> That sweet fruit whereof the care of mortals
> goeth in search on so many boughs.[23]

When and where have we known happiness, for us to have so lively a wish for it from our very birth? In a former life? But this would merely be to displace the problem into our previous life; it would not solve it. We bear, inscribed within us, the wish to be happy because God has created us 'in his own image and like-ness', and he himself, being perfect happiness, has made us for happiness as well. The desire for happiness is kneaded into us.

If that is so, how is it so few people are truly happy, and even those who are are so for such a little while? I say again: we are climbing the wrong side. We have chosen a slope that doesn't lead to the peak. Prints, paintings and photographs survive from the end of the last century and the beginning of our own, depicting famous accidents on the Matterhorn: whole groups of mountaineers roped together and crashing down the rocks. As though the mountain, feeling irritable, were shaking these rash creatures off its back. It is an image of what happens on the climb to happiness.

Not hard to discover where the error lurks. Revelation tells us: 'God is love'; we human beings have thought we could reverse the phrase and say: love is God! Again, revelation tells us: 'God is happiness'; again we human beings invert the order and say: happiness is God! But what happens then? We do not know pure, absolute, eternal and transcendent happiness, any more than we know absolute love. We know fragments of happiness, which often amount to a passing intoxication of the senses. Tinsel joys which dazzle us for a moment with their splendour but contain the tormenting potential of going to bits from one minute to the next. On this tack, we divinize our own experiences. The work of our hands or of our brains we call 'God'. The ancients made no bones of making happiness a goddess, whom they aptly named *Felicitas*. Such in substance is the joy celebrated by Beethoven at the end of the Ninth Symphony: 'spark of the Gods, daughter of Elysium'. A joy which is not enough for all, but is reserved rather for 'the man who has had a good wife and known good friends', as the ode says further on.

This explains why those who seek God always find joy, while those who seek joy do not always find God. Those who seek joy rather than God, outside God, find nothing but a vain simulacrum of it, a 'dry wet-nurse', 'cracked water tanks that hold no water' (Jeremiah 2:13). And so we are reduced to seeking happiness by way of quantity: by chasing after pleasures and emotions ever more intense, or by adding pleasure to pleasure. But we ourselves experience the fact that 'eyes have never had

enough of seeing, nor ears their fill of hearing' (Ecclesiastes 1:18).
Throughout his life, Dr Faustus sought for a moment so beautiful
that it would wrench the cry: 'Stay!' from his lips. He never finds
it and this precisely is what in the end will save him. 'No good or
pleasure has ever satisfied him,' in vexation says the Enemy of his
soul.[24]

We need to make the leap from quantity to quality of joy.
Only God is happy and makes others happy. That is why a psalm
exhorts us to 'make the Lord your joy and he will give you your
heart's desires' (Psalm 37:4). With him too, the joys of this
present life retain their sweet savour and do not turn into afflic-
tions. Only he has power to wrench from the lips of a saint the
cry: 'Enough of joy, Lord; my heart can contain no more of it!'
The Bible describes eternal life in the imagery of the banquet, of
the wedding feast, of song and dance: all things that speak to us
of happiness. Entering into this is to make our final entry into joy:
'Come and join in your Master's happiness' (Matthew 25:21).

In God is found everything we are accustomed to associate
with the word happiness and infinitely more, for 'what no eye has
seen and no ear has heard, what the human mind cannot visualize: all this God has prepared for those who love him' (cf. 1
Corinthians 2:9). The finishing post Christianity points us the
way to is not the simple cessation of pain, the extinguishing of
our desires. It is infinitely more: it is the fulfilment of all desires:
'Unbounded joy in your presence,' says one of the psalms, 'at
your right hand delight for ever' (Psalm 16:11).

We live, it has been said, in an age of anxiety. The concept of
anxiety has taken the place occupied in ancient thought by that of
happiness. Anxiety has invaded philosophy, psychology, literature. Were we, years hence, to try and form an idea of how people
lived in the twentieth century and were to take a writer such as
Franz Kafka for instance as our baseline, we should carry away
the impression of a mortal anxiety which had seeped into every

crevice of human life. All these speeches on the unhappiness of
the human condition do however tell us one thing at least: that
we are not resigned to being unhappy, that we feel it to be alien,
unnatural. The struggle against anxiety is another way of bearing
witness to the irrepressible need we have to be happy.

Now is the time for us to start boldly proclaiming the 'glad
tidings' that God is happiness, that happiness – not suffering,
privation and the cross – will have the last word. That suffering
serves merely to remove the obstacle to joy, to dilate the soul for
it to entertain as much joy as possible. That the joy that comes
from God is such as to triumph even while we are still undergoing
trials here below. As Nehemiah said to the weeping people: 'The
joy of the Lord is your strength' (Nehemiah 8:10).

What should be the cry with which to close our tortured
millennium and prepare ourselves for the next? The note to be
imprinted on the new evangelization? The human race has now
become convinced that we have to choose between God and
happiness. We have unwittingly made God the rival, the enemy,
of human joy. An 'envious' God, like that of certain pagan
writers. But this is Satan's work *par excellence*, the weapon he
successfully used with Eve.

After this, we can pursue our way with a new certainty
lending wings to our feet: our climb towards the Living God is
also a climb towards happiness. But up the right side.

Let us close with one of the Church's prayers:

> O God, you unite the hearts of all your faithful. Teach us to
> love what you command and to long for what you promise,
> so that amid the delights of this life we may keep our hearts
> set firmly on the true joys of heaven.[25]

4   A terrible and fascinating mystery

We have already said we can't define the Living God. But we can at least say how and where to find him. One night, having spent longer than usual at prayer, the philosopher Pascal underwent a burning experience of the Living God. And this he did his best to record, in the form of brief exclamations, on a piece of vellum which, after his death, was found stitched inside his jerkin, over his heart. It said:

> God of Abraham, God of Isaac, God of Jacob, not of the philosophers and savants. Certitude. Certitude. Feeling. Joy. Peace. God of Jesus Christ. 'Thy God shall be my God.' Forgetfulness of the world and of everything except God. He is to be found only in the ways taught in the Gospel. Grandeur of the human soul. 'Righteous Father, the world has not known Thee, but I have known Thee.' May I never fall away from him for ever. Joy, joy, tears of joy.

Here we can see, from life, what it means to discover that God exists and 'to have one's breath taken away'.

One phrase in Pascal's text is of particular interest to us here. The Living God 'is to be found only in the ways of the Gospel', that is to say, in the Bible. (He also makes the point in practical terms by expressing himself very largely in quotations from the Bible.) The Living God 'walks' in the Scriptures, just as we read he walked in the Garden of Eden at the beginning of the world (cf. Genesis 3:8). We meet him there at every step. 'What does it mean,' asks St Ambrose,

> that God walked in the garden, when he is always every-
> where? I think it means this: God may be said to walk wher-
> ever throughout the Scriptures his presence is implied.[26]

Let us then do as Moses did. Let us hide in a cleft of the rock – in a certain page of Scripture, that is to say – so as to catch, at least by reflection and fleetingly, some flash of his glory and some manifestation of his life. True it is, we can't describe the Living God or contain him in a set of definitions, 'but,' says St Cyril of Jerusalem,

> though it is true I can't drink all the water in a river, must I,
> because this is so, die of thirst? Going into a garden, even
> though I can't eat all the fruit inside, does this mean I must go
> away as hungry as before?[27]

Let us take God's judgments, for instance. The Bible speaks of God's judgments very frequently, proclaiming them to be just, holy, inscrutable, terrible and, at the same time 'sweeter than honey that drips from the comb' (Psalm 19:10). 'How rich and deep are the wisdom and the knowledge of God! We cannot reach the root of his judgments or his ways!' (Romans 11:33). 'The towns of Judah exult', says one of the psalms, 'because of your judgments' (Psalm 97:8), and again: 'Your judgments are like the mighty deep' (Psalm 36:6).

In the idea of God constructed by the philosophers, this finds no counterpart; you would never imagine such judgments exist, that the whole world, as one psalmist says, is full of his judgments (cf. Psalm 105:7). God's judgments are something very different from the Platonic ideals contained in God's mind. They are at once thoughts and decisions, creative thoughts which 'decide' the fate of human beings and the course of history. How sobering it is to consider that we are ever under the judgment of God! That all is bare and open to him, not least the thoughts of those who deny him. 'O Lord,' says the author of *The Imitation of Christ*,

> thou thunderest thy judgments upon me and shakest all my bones with fear and trembling, and my soul is greatly terrified. I stand astonished and reflect that 'the heavens are not pure in thy sight'.[28]

The Living God reveals himself above all in the most mysterious of his judgments: that which is manifested in the cross of Christ. But to discover what new factor the cross contributes to our understanding of the Living God, we must call some powerful moments to mind in the biblical revelation of God.

In the Book of Exodus, God introduces himself to Moses by saying: 'The Lord, the Lord!' Then follow two sets of attributes:

> God of tenderness and compassion, slow to anger, rich in faithful love and constancy, maintaining his faithful love to thousands, forgiving fault, crime and sin . . . but letting nothing go unchecked, and punishing the parents' fault in the children and in the grandchildren to the third and fourth generation (Exodus 34:6–7).

This characteristic contrast is preserved throughout the Bible.

The psalms sing now the one, now the other, of these aspects: now the God who forgives, now the God who punishes. There is a psalm entitled 'Hymn to God the Terrible' in which God is said to be radiant, awe-inspiring, irresistible; 'he cuts short the breath of princes' (Psalm 76) and there is another psalm in which the same God is said to be 'tenderness and pity, slow to anger, full of faithful love' and that 'his tenderness embraces all his creatures' (Psalm 145:8–9).

To indicate an infinite reality, we have no better resource than to make use of opposites and to speak by contradictions. Thus, to say what the Holy Spirit is, we use two symbols which are diametrically opposed to one another: water and fire. Of Jesus Christ we say he is at once lamb and lion (cf. Revelation 5:5–6). Opposites have the power to create an open, infinite space between them. The Bible consistently maintains, together, in tension, these two fundamental characteristics of God: on the one hand, holiness and power; on the other, immense kindness; on the one hand, anger; on the other, compassion. It makes no effort to level them out, it never sees a contradiction between them. And correspondingly we see the two reactions or attitudes, and as well the basic duties, of the creature before this God: fear and love: 'You must love the Lord your God . . . You must fear the Lord your God' (Deuteronomy 6:5, 13).

All the great experiences of the Living God display these two contrasting characteristics of God, maintaining them in balance. Mary, in the *Magnificat* calls God: 'Lord', 'Almighty', 'Holy', all titles expressing majesty, transcendence, and arousing reverence and fear; but she also calls him 'my Saviour', a title expressing kindness, condescension, and inspiring love and trust. St Francis of Assisi begins his *Canticle of the Creatures* by calling God 'Most high, almighty and good Lord . . .' and by saying that no one is fit 'to mention' him; in another prayer he calls him 'Almighty, eternal, just and merciful God . . . !' For him therefore

God is 'most high, almighty, eternal, just', but at the same time 'good and merciful'!

St Augustine better than anyone else has illustrated this twofold, contrasting, human reaction of love and fear, of which we have been speaking: 'When first I knew you,' he says, having returned to God, 'you raised me up. Blazing upon me with your rays, you struck down my feeble gaze, and I trembled with love and awe.' At the presence of God, he says elsewhere, 'I am both terrified and set on fire'.[29]

Taking this fact as his basis, a well-known exponent of the phenomenology of religion has developed his thesis on the divine as a mystery at once 'terrible and fascinating', that is to say, terrifying by its power and attracting by its goodness. He sees this same fundamental conception of God as being present in the most disparate of religious systems, both ancient and modern, even though he grants the highest expression of that mystery to reside in Christianity because of its moral content.[30]

Not always, truth to tell, even among Christians have people managed to maintain a proper balance between these opposites. There have been trends in spirituality (most frequently of Catholic origin) putting so much emphasis on the aspect of goodness and condescension (*le bon Dieu*!) as to leave that of God's majesty and of holy fear of God in the shade; and there have been trends (the best-known of them deriving from Calvin) which have put so much stress on the crushing majesty, power and glory of God as to leave us with fear as almost our only possible reaction. 'When we reflect on the terrible majesty of God, it is impossible', he says, 'not to be terrified by it. Fear is the foundation of religion.'

Before pursuing our argument any further, let us now pray in the words of St Francis of Assisi:

Lord, may we grow in our knowledge of you,
so that we may appreciate
the width of your favours,
the length of your promises,
the sublimity of your majesty
and the depth of your judgments. Amen.[31]

5   I hate your works,
        I love you

People sometimes think that, in the Gospel, Jesus had finally resolved the tension between these two characteristics of the Godhead, in favour of a God exclusively good, tender, fatherly, who never gets angry, never strikes with dread. A God who is only infinite love and not infinite power as well. The first person to teach this as a system was Marcion. 'Marcion', says St Irenaeus,

> divides God in two, saying that the one is good and the other
> apt to judge. But in so doing he destroys the one and the
> other, for a God who judges, if not also good, is not God, nor
> is a God who is good but inapt to judge.[32]

Marcion's thesis was taken up by the Cathars in the Middle Ages and, in more recent times and in a toned-down form, by Simone Weil. The result is, every time, to detach the New Testament from the Old, as though the former belonged to a different God, one hitherto unknown.

But this way of seeing things doesn't do justice either to the Old Testament or to the New. The idea of an Old Testament God who is only severity and justice arouses the justified protests of our Jewish brothers as taking no account of the expressions of consuming fatherly tenderness put into God's mouth by the prophets (cf. Jeremiah 31:20; Hosea 11:8–9). Equally ill-founded is the thesis that the God of the Gospel knows nothing but goodness and indulgence.

Jesus bids us fear the God who can condemn to hell. He foretells a judgment at which he himself will be the judge and will utter the terrible: 'Depart from me, accursed ones . . .' Paul too was to speak of the wrath of God (cf. Romans 1:18) and another New Testament book was to say: 'It is a dreadful thing to fall into the hands of the Living God' (Hebrews 10:31).

The novelty Jesus embodies is something quite different. It is that God, while remaining what he was, i.e. the God thrice-holy, most high and almighty, has now been given to us in a new way, as father, or rather as *abba*, daddy. No slack or mawkish idea of God. The prayer of the 'Our Father' itself embraces these two aspects of God. For the words 'Our Father' express the infinite condescension, nearness, goodness, fatherliness of God. God is 'father', and he is 'ours'. But the words 'who art in heaven' contrastingly express distance, transcendence, holiness.[33] The expression 'in heaven' doesn't indicate place but condition of existence. It amounts to saying that God is spirit, not flesh, that he is most high, that he is as far from us 'as the heavens are high above the earth' (cf. Isaiah 55:9).

The greatness and novelty of Jesus's revelation of God can be summed up thus: We have a God for our father! We have a father for our God! The Church has faithfully taken on board this antinomic picture of God, saying at the beginning of her Creed: 'I believe in God the Father almighty'. Father, but almighty; almighty, yet Father.

But more than by words, Jesus brings the revelation of the Living God to completion by an event: his death on the cross. The Crucified is the supreme manifestation of the Living God; it is, be it said, the supreme judgment of God in history. Not for nothing does the Book of Revelation, when speaking of the cross, call it 'the seal of the Living God' (Revelation 7:2).

Seeing the twofold series of manifestations of the Living God, some people might take offence at a God who now punishes, now forgives, is now in a rage, is now all goodness, and think we have a capricious and arbitrary being to deal with, or an unpredictable one at best. Indeed this risk is by no means avoided in such religious phenomenological reconstructions as the one mentioned above. There, the only explanation lies in the concept of the irrational. God contains within himself a rational aspect, one we can understand, and an irrational aspect which cannot be resolved by rational categories but only by other categories and other symbols.

Jesus on the cross is the true key for solving this ambiguity. God is not severe and compassionate by turns, depending on his whim. He doesn't bring his omnipotence and mercy into play turn and turn about, arbitrarily, without sound reasons. There is an explanation for this ambivalence and this is it: God is good, tender with the sinner; he is holy, terrible and implacable against sin. 'I hate what you do; I love you' an Augustinian maxim would have God say (*Odi tua, amo te*). God hates or spurns nothing that he has made (cf. Wisdom 11:21–26). One thing he hates and hounds 'for a thousand generations' that is to say, down to its remotest consequences, something he has not made, something he has not willed: evil. But evil is what primarily destroys the creature. So his anger against sin is an anger against a common enemy, since he is love. So when we hear these words from God's mouth: 'Though I struck you in anger, in mercy I have pitied you' (Isaiah 60:10), we can now grasp what they really mean: 'I have struck your wrongdoing, out of compassion for you.'

In what sense then is Jesus on the cross the supreme revelation of the Living God in the Bible? In the sense that the cross is the most terrible *No* to sin and the most loving *Yes* to the sinner. St Paul says that God treated Jesus as sin for our sake, so that we might become righteous and holy, that is to say, be loved by God (cf. 2 Corinthians 5:21). He 'condemned sin in the flesh of Christ' to save sinners in this fashion (cf. Romans 8:3–4). Omnipotence and love are not in opposition to each other, not even juxtaposed or wisely rationed out, but in vital relationship with one another: God shows his omnipotence by being compassionate!

Thus justice and peace have kissed each other on Christ's cross; God's holiness and his love for us have met there. In contemplating Christ on the cross from now on, we come to know the Living God, and this explains why he is so easily lost to view by those who seek him only in books and in philosophical systems. The very expression 'theology of the cross' (*theologia crucis*) implies that from now onwards one cannot talk about God (that is, literally: theologize), unless one starts from the cross. 'One does not become a theologian by understanding, reading and speculating, but by living or better still dying, experiencing what it is to be put to death.'[34] In other words, by living the mystery of the cross.

The Bible goes much further, as we see, than the simple phenomenological statement that God is a terrible and fascinating mystery!

Even before Christ's death on the cross, there is his birth, inaugurating a new phase in our knowledge of the Living God. Together, incarnation and paschal mystery have profoundly modified our relationship with the Living God, by making idolatry for ever out-of-date and 'inexcusable'. God has himself made an image of himself. For Christ is 'the image of the unseen God' (Colossians 1:15). An image not made with a different substance – marble, stone or whatever other created thing – but with the actual substance of God. A 'consubstantial' image, as the Council of Nicaea was to state and as we repeat in the Creed. For the Son is 'the reflection of the Father's glory and the imprint of his substance' (Hebrews 1:3).

To Jesus' question: 'Who do you say I am?' Peter replies: 'You are the Christ, the Son of the Living God' (Matthew 16:15–16). The Living God is now represented, 'live', on earth by the Son. There is no further need for substitutes. God from now on will not be known from images made by human hand but by the image he has made of himself, no longer by an idea, but by a reality. 'God who said: "Let light shine out of darkness", has shone into our hearts to enlighten them with the knowledge of God's glory, the glory on the face of Christ' (2 Corinthians 4:6). The divine glory which long ago no one could look upon and stay alive (cf. Exodus 33:18ff), may now be contemplated by everyone on earth.

Let us pray with the Church:

> O God, you reveal your almighty power
> above all in your mercy and forbearance;
> fill our hearts with your grace
> so that nothing may hold us back
> from the joys of heaven
> which you have promised us.
> Through Christ our Lord.[35]

6   God, the eternal rock

We have tried to arouse the 'feeling' of the Living God in ourselves by considering his 'judgments'. That same feeling can also be provoked, as we have said, by way of analogy and contrast. One biblical image which speaks this way to us about God is the image of the rock. Here the most material and static of things stands for the most spiritual and dynamic of realities (this is the contrast); the most enduring and impressive of things stands for him who is the Unchangeable, the Strong (this is the analogy). Few biblical titles can arouse such a vivid, even if unanalysed, feeling of God – above all of what God is for us – as this one of God as rock. Let us too, as Scripture bids us, try to suck ·'honey from the rock' (cf. Deuteronomy 32:13).

    In the Bible, rather than a mere title, 'rock' seems to be a sort of personal name of God's, and hence is sometimes written with a capital letter. 'He is the Rock, perfect is his work' (Deuteronomy 32:4); 'The Lord is an eternal rock' (Isaiah 26:4). But why this image doesn't inspire us with fear and uneasiness by the hardness and impenetrability it evokes is because the Bible immediately adds another truth: he is 'our' rock, 'my' rock. That is to say, a rock on our side, not one against us. 'The Lord is my rock' (Psalm 18:2), the 'rock of my defence' (Psalm 31:3), the 'rock of our salvation' (Psalm 95:1). The earliest translators of the Bible, the Seventy, jibbed at such a material image of God as seeming to debase him, and systematically for concrete 'rock' substituted abstract nouns like 'strength', 'refuge', 'salvation'. But all modern translations, I'm glad to say, have now given God back his original title 'Rock'.

When, climbing up from the valley and having negotiated the pass, I first saw the Matterhorn outlined against the sky, I instantly grasped what the Bible intended to convey to us in calling God 'the rock'. As we stand before that pyramid of rock rearing up, alone, in an almost supernatural way, against the blue of the sky, we feel like midgets and are seized with a strange kind of humility. We gaze in silence, saying nothing. But the Matterhorn stood there, unmoving, while we made our way down again, carrying away with us only the impression and the memory consigned to a photograph. Not so with this other rock. It, if we wish it, will follow us, we can carry it in our heart. It is written of the rock from which water gushed in the desert that it 'accompanied' the people (cf. 1 Corinthians 10:4). So it is with God.

True, that to discover the significance of God as rock, we must first have experienced this: that everything passes. Day passes, minute by minute, and suddenly it's evening. Trees flower, then bear fruit, then lose their leaves and it's winter again. Then comes the time when the tree itself grows old and falls. As with objects, so with us. 'We are like the leaves on the trees in autumn.'[36] In an effort not to pass away, not to die entirely, we cling now to youth, now to love, now to our children, now to fame, thinking thus to erect 'monuments more lasting than bronze'. But in vain. At the very moment of birth begins the countdown that nothing, night and day, can halt. 'Human life is but a puff of wind' (Psalm 144:4).

How do human beings react to this universal experience that everything passes away? Before Christ, there were opposing responses to it. One philosopher, Parmenides, said that everything is immutable and that change is only apparent; in a word, that nothing really passes away. After him, another philosopher, Heraclitus, said the opposite: that nothing is unchanging in the world, that everything is in flux. To him was attributed the famous phrase *panta rei*, 'everything flows'. After these two, a third thinker, Empedocles of Agrigentum tried to reconcile the two extremes. It is true, he said, that everything flows, but there is something permanent beneath the incessant flow of all things. He called this something the 'One', the 'Sphere' or the 'divine generative Power'. He could not say more than this and so fell into not a few contradictions. But even so, he won his place in what the Fathers used to call 'the preparation for the Gospel'. Confusedly he had glimpsed that truth clearly stated in the Bible, where God is called 'the eternal rock'. In nature, the rock represents that which rears up, immutable, amid all geological and atmospheric changes occurring in the landscape around it.

> They pass away but you remain;
> they all wear out like a garment,
> like worn-out clothes you change them.
> But you remain the same (Psalm 102:26).

Possibly impressed by the contrast between the sands of the desert and the rocks of the Sinai *massif*, the poets of Israel saw this as symbolizing the difference between human beings and God. We are 'like dust'; God is an 'eternal rock'! St Teresa of Avila encapsulated this particular feeling about God in some lapidary phrases:

> Let nothing disturb you, let nothing affright you. Everything
> passes, God alone remains. Patience overcomes all things.
> Whoever has God wants for nothing. God alone is enough.

Also, in respect of God as rock, the coming of Christ creates a fundamentally new departure. No longer can one talk of God and stop short of Christ or leave him out, without mutilating the revelation about God. 'That rock was Christ,' says St Paul while speaking of the rock that 'accompanied' the Israelites in the desert (cf. 1 Corinthians 10:4). The inaccessible rock made itself accessible and visible in the Word, who came to dwell among us. The 'cleft in the rock' where Moses sheltered so that he could gaze at God (cf. Exodus 33:22) prefigured, according to the Fathers, Christ's human nature, which allows us to enter into contact with God without being destroyed by his glory. Whence the invitation that St Bonaventure and other saints address to souls athirst for God, to stay like doves 'in the crevices of the rock' (Song of Songs 2:14), that is to say, within Christ's wounded side.[37]

Having risen from the dead, Christ in a new way became the rock that 'accompanies' us through history. Whoever builds on his word builds on rock (cf. Matthew 7:24). He is 'the cornerstone' on which the Church is founded (cf. Ephesians 2:20); the rejected stone that has become the cornerstone (1 Peter 2:7); the 'rock of offence' or stumbling-block for those who turn him down (Romans 9:32f). In a new way, the eternal Rock has become 'our rock', 'the rock of our salvation'.

Rock is not an abstract title, it doesn't merely say what God is, but also what we ourselves ought to be. The rock is meant to be climbed, where we can seek refuge and not merely gaze at it from afar. The rock attracts and thrills. If God is rock, human beings should be rock climbers. One might even conceive of a very special club: The Friends of the Rock Club. Jesus said:

'Learn from the householder'; 'Look at the fishermen'. St James goes on to say: 'Look at the farmers'. We may add: 'Look at the rock climbers'! Rock climbers do not entrust their weight to bushes sprouting out of some crevice, they do not choose well-trodden paths, even if these are easier to climb. If darkness falls or a storm blows up, they don't take the rash course of trying to climb on up, but cling even tighter to the rock and wait until the storm is over. Rock climbers hold fast to the rock, they stick to it with hands and feet, they are literally nailed to the rock. And this is what we too must be with our rock. The surest way of sticking to this rock is to cling to the cross, to be 'fixed to the cross with Christ' (Galatians 2:20). Clinging to him, the living stone, we too shall become 'living stones' (cf. 1 Peter 2:5). Little rocks.

There is a psalm which tells of the vicissitudes of a believer who was on the point of forsaking God, 'seeing the prosperity of the wicked'. But on reflection, he realized he had got the wrong idea: the godless are in fact on slippery ground, they hurtle to their doom, pass away in a flash. Then he grasps what it means to be founded on the rock and exclaims: 'My heart's rock, my portion, God for ever . . . My happiness is to be near God. I have made the Lord my refuge' (Psalm 73). This is the best definition of faith, if it is true that originally 'I believe' (*credo*) meant 'to set your heart on something'.

It certainly creates an impression if you think of a heart set on a rock: the tenderest of things in contact with the hardest. But rock climbers will know how to reply to this too. Those who spend days and nights in contact with the rock, who entrust their lives to the rock, will eventually come to know every cranny in it. Under their fingers the rock as it were comes alive, responds, becomes living rock. When speaking of the rock they become poets. So too, the rock which is God is a living, pulsating rock. A rock of tenderness. That is why another psalmist can exclaim: 'I love you, Lord, my rock!' (Psalm 18:1). The only time in the Bible when anyone says 'I love you' to God (and not, as usually is the case, when God says this to a human being), he is addressing God as rock.

The Bible's insistence on God as rock has the purpose of infusing confidence in the creature, of driving out fears from our heart. 'We shall not be afraid though the earth be in turmoil, though mountains tumble into the depths of the sea', says a psalm; and the reason given is this: 'Our fortified rock is the God of Jacob' (Psalm 46:3, 7). Such is the state of soul expressed in the hymn 'A safe stronghold our God is still', which has played so important a role in moulding religious sentiment in the Protestant world.[38] One fear alone remains before this God-rock; yet it isn't properly speaking fear, but awe: holy awe of God.

The revelation of God-rock should end with an existential decision: to approach it, climb it, 'to stablish one's own feet on the rock'. We know the word 'Pasch' means 'passing' and that passing, in itself, is a negative thing, indicating transience, instability. Would the Pasch then be the sacrament of transience, an umpteenth confirmation that 'everything passes'? On the contrary, the Pasch or Passover does indeed mean a passing over, but a passing over 'from this world to the Father' (cf. John 13:1), that is to say, from the instability of this world to the super-solid kingdom of God. Precisely so as not to pass away with this world, we pass over to the rock that remains for ever. All of us, good and bad, will certainly pass away, but it is one thing to pass away 'from' the world and another to pass away 'with' the world. 'The world, with all its disordered desires, is passing away, but whoever does the will of God remains for ever' (1 John 2:17).

With the Church, let us pray:

> Grant us, Lord, always to revere and love your holy name; for you never withdraw your guidance from those you have firmly established on the solid rock of your love.[39]

7 The heavens declare the glory of God

Now we must open the wide-angle lens on God, I mean the heavens themselves. There is a psalm which begins as follows:

> The heavens declare the glory of God,
> the vault of heaven proclaims his handiwork (Psalm 19).

God has written two books: the one is Scripture; the other, the creation. One is made up of letters and words, the other of things. Not everyone can or knows how to read the book of Scripture, but all of us, even the illiterate, can read the book that is the created world. From every point on earth, by night even better than by day. 'From the entire earth the design stands out, this message reaches the whole world' (Psalm 19:4). The book lies open wide to the eyes of all, like one of those enormous parchment psalters with big lettering and Gregorian notes in white and red, which used to stand on a lectern in the middle of the choir, so that all the monks could read and sing while each stayed in his stall.

God didn't create the natural world so as then to go away and disappear. In a certain sense he is hidden in it, under veils as it were, and hence, when contemplating the creation, we can detect traces of him. 'Ever since the creation of the world, the invisible existence of God and his everlasting power have been clearly seen by the mind's understanding of created things' (Romans 1:20).

So many people have heard that silent 'message' of the heavens and, thanks to it, have had their earliest intuition of the mystery of God or have had their faith strengthened, if already believers. Let us pause then for a moment to hear what the natural world has to say. Hitherto we have sought the Living God in the Scriptures, now let us seek him in creation too.

What are the heavens saying in their unending proclamation? First and foremost, that God exists. The entire firmament is a burning bush from which God ceaselessly proclaims his name: 'I am here!' We ought not to silence this 'classic' argument for the existence of God or be nervous about trotting it out as though it were too simple, too ingenuous for people today. Or as though it were already refuted by someone or other and the matter settled once and for all by modern 'critical reason', whereas the truth is that no one has ever been able to silence that voice. It is still the argument which has most effect on those whose hearts are free of prejudice and whose eyes, like those of a child, are open to wonder. Of all kinds of knowledge, writes Kant, himself the philosopher of critical reason, the most important is this: that God exists; and hence Providence has not willed to base this knowledge on the subtleties of philosophic arguments but has entrusted it to the natural, ordinary intelligence, when this is not perverted. Kant himself confessed that two things above all filled him with ever new wonder and reverence: the starry sky above him and the moral conscience within him.[40] So much so that he wished to have these words carved on his tomb once he was dead.

Who arranges that millions and millions of heavenly bodies

don't founder in chaos from second to second, but instead wheel round in such perfect, unchanging harmony? That the planets in their orbits go fast enough to escape the fatal pull of the sun, but not so fast as to part company with it and get lost in icy space? In a word, how can we explain 'universal harmony' and not admit a governing intelligence above the universe? No one seeing so many thousands of aircraft in the world all taking off and landing at fixed times every day, streaking through the heavens in all directions without colliding, each following its own route at its particular altitude, would think all this could be happening by chance without anyone's having agreed on a timetable or drawn up a plan and regulations. And yet what is this air traffic in comparison with what goes on in space? To say all that is due to chance or unknown cosmic laws means either that we're closing our eyes to the problem or that we're merely giving God a different name and calling him 'Chance' or 'Cosmic Laws'.

Our friend the poet Péguy is right in saying that believing is relatively easy and hoping is really what is hard: 'I have no problem with belief,' says God.

> I shine so brightly in my creation – in sun and moon and stars, in the planets in the vault of heaven, and in the fish in the sea – that, not to believe, those poor wretches (he is speaking of us) would have to be blind. To believe, you have only to let yourself go, you only have to look. So as not to believe, you would have to force yourself, torture, torment, thwart yourself, become rigid. Turn yourself back to front.[41]

Unfortunately, this turning oneself back to front, this going against oneself, is precisely what we are doing to ourselves today, complicated and contorted as we are by our own scientific progress.

But this is only the start of what the heavens are telling. That is the message for the beginners. The heavens proclaim not only the *existence* of God (for this in fact they take for granted); they also proclaim his *glory*. That is to say, his magnificence, his splendour. To them is entrusted the revelation of one very particular aspect of God: his infinity. The human body, the flowers, the colours, a single leaf: all these alone suffice to proclaim the inexhaustible beauty, riches and imagination of God. But who will also proclaim his vastness and greatness? Religiously speaking, this is the task the universe in its immensity discharges.

I still have a childhood memory vividly in mind. One summer day, having got too hot, I lay on my back in the grass to rest. Above me the immense blue vault of the sky with thin, very white, unmoving clouds. I began to wonder: what's above that blue vault? and what's above that? An impression of boundless space and infinite silence filled my mind. Mystery. That was my earliest intimation of the infinite and the eternal.

Contemplation of the firmament has the power to carry our mind to its furthest bounds, on the threshold of shipwreck and surrender. It makes us giddy. The Milky Way alone contains not less than a hundred billion stars, and to think that our most powerful telescopes can scan at least ten billion galaxies like our own! The most distant star we know is fourteen billion light-years away from us; now, to have some idea of what this means, you have only to think that the sun – which is some hundred and fifty million kilometres away from earth – takes little more than eight minutes to send its light to us.

Yes, faced with the size of the universe, 'to the high fantasy power fails'.[42] Our imagination cannot conceive what expressions like 'billions of light-years' can mean. We are reduced to helplessness, humility. 'I look up to your heavens, shaped by your fingers, at the moon and stars you set firm – what are human beings that you spare a thought for them?' (Psalm 8:3–4). So is born that characteristic sense of wonder which almost always prepares the way for and accompanies faith.

Sometimes, when considering the 'astronomical' figures of the universe, we are seized with a kind of dismay and almost outrage. 'Why all this waste?' we too are tempted to ask (cf. Matthew 26:6ff). And consequently the conviction is gaining ground that living and intelligent beings also exist in other parts of the universe. 'Biochemical and biological considerations,' we read, 'together with statistical considerations on the number of galaxies, permit us to suppose the existence of vegetable, animal and even intelligent life in the universe to be very probable.'

But is this a necessary hypothesis and is there any point in this case of calculating the probabilities and statistical laws? Isn't the same disproportion and prodigality of the Creator also to be observed on earth? How many 'useless' species and as well as these, the flowers, plants, fish, insects! And what about human spermatozoa? Each time nature squanders tens and tens of millions of spermatozoa while only a single one of them gets used and is sufficient to generate a new human life. Life and conscious- ness being of so different and superior an order, nature, so to speak, spares no expense to ensure success.

But here is the most important point for us. If the heavens declare the glory of God, what will our task on earth be, if not to echo the cosmic choir? 'Heaven and earth are full of his glory.' They are, in a manner of speaking, heavy with it. But on their own, they cannot discharge their burden. Like a pregnant woman, they too need the skilled hands of the midwife to bring out that with which they are 'full'. And midwife to God's glory is what we must be. How long the universe has had to wait, what a long run-up there has had to be, before reaching this point! Millions and billions of years while matter painfully advanced through opacity towards the light of consciousness, just as the sap rises from the subsoil to the tree-top, there to expand in flower and fruit. This consciousness was reached at last when in the universe appeared 'the phenomenon of man'.

But now that the universe has reached its goal, it requires human beings to do their duty, which is that we, in a manner of speaking, assume direction of the choir and lead the rest in 'Glory to God in the highest!' 'When, while I am saying Mass,' said the Blessed Heinrich Suso,

> I reach the words *Sursum corda*, I imagine I have before me all the beings created by God in heaven and earth: water, air, fire, light, and each element, each with its own name; so too the birds of the air, the fish in the sea and the flowers in the woods, all the herbs and plants of the countryside, the count-less sands of the sea, the grains of dust we see in the shafts of sunlight, the raindrops that have fallen or are about to fall, the beads of dew that deck the meadow. Then I imagine myself to be in the midst of these creatures, like a choir-master surrounded by a boundless choir.

By observing the universe, someone of religious temperament is not only taught to praise, but also to obey. In the stars we perceive a marvellous, even if unconscious, example of joyful obedience.

> God sends the light – and it goes; he recalls it – and trembling it obeys; the stars shine joyfully at their posts; when he calls them, they answer, 'Here we are'. They shine to delight their Creator (Baruch 3:33–5).

I know of a man who was training to become an aircraft pilot; he studied astronomy, trigonometry and all the sciences teaching one how to travel the heavens and how, if need be, to check one's route by the stars. One day he happened to read our psalm: 'The heavens declare the glory of God ...' Instantly scales fell from his eyes. So the sky he had been studying so keenly was not there merely to provide him with a sort of set of celestial traffic signs. There was infinitely more in it to be discovered. The glory of God was there! This expression now seemed to contain worlds unexplored, which one might spend a lifetime investigating. The man in question now, when not piloting aircraft through the sky, goes about with other members of a Christian lay community, proclaiming the God of Jesus Christ.

Let us close by calling to mind the prayer with which the famous astronomer Kepler concluded his work *De Harmonice Mundi*:

> Great is the Lord and great his power,
> his wisdom has no bounds.
> Praise him, heavens, sun, moon, planets,
> whatever be the tongue you use to praise your Creator.
> Praise him, too, my soul.
> From him, through him and in him are all things,
> as well those of which we know nothing
> as those which we know, which are a minute part.
> To him be praise, honour and glory for ever and ever. Amen.[43]

8   Return into yourself

St Paul says that in this world we see God 'as in a mirror' (1 Corinthians 13:12). This mirror is, in different ways, Scripture and nature (the two books!), but above all it is our own soul. At the foot of the Dolomites we often meet with little lakes in which the white mountains are reflected so clearly that, in a photograph, it's hard to be sure which is the actual mountain and which the reflection. Our souls are like these little lakes: in each, the entire reality of God is reflected, the whole Trinity. I speak of 'soul', even though I know today people hardly talk of it any more, preferring at most to talk of 'psyche' for fear of seeming too religiose.

We cannot know God outside ourselves – in Scripture and in the creation – if in some way, however imperfect, we do not also know him within ourselves. That is the true meeting place between God and human nature. And the reason is a simple one. God created men and women – and them alone – 'in his own image and likeness' (Genesis 1:26). Like is not known except by like, and the human soul alone in the material world bears a likeness to God. To this basic reason, which originates from the creation, is added another no less cogent, derived from the redemption, i.e. that in baptism we have become 'the temple of God' (1 Corinthians 3:16).

The mere existence of the soul is the best proof that God exists. If, as to the psalmist in foreign exile, a non-believer should say to me: 'Where is your God?' (Psalm 42:3), I answer back: 'Where is your soul? Show me your soul, if you can, and I will show you my God. You say: "I will show you my soul by its effects, since even though I can't see it or touch it, I can indeed see that it acts. At its nod, the limbs of my body move; I am silent or I speak as my soul commands me." So it is with my God, I reply to you, I can see him in the things he has done and is constantly doing in the world: things for which he is the only adequate explanation.'

So St Augustine sets out his programme for seeking God, by saying: 'It is by my soul that I shall ascend to him.' Among the various faculties of the soul, he believes he can perceive God above all in memory.

> What resting-place have you fashioned for yourself? What sanctuary have you built for yourself? . . . This is where I keep finding you, whenever I remember you.[44]

And after Augustine, the exponents of Rhineland mysticism were to attempt to excavate even further in depth into the recesses of the soul, in search of the meeting place with God; and this they perceived to be in the so-called 'depths of the soul' from which memory, intelligence and will emanate and into which they flow back into unity.

When however we creatures actually manage to attain, to some degree, this God 'within the self', we realize that he transcends us; that he is not contained within the soul but that he contains it. This is why the images of 'depth' or 'abyss' alternate with those of 'peak' or 'tip' of the soul, beyond which one must fling oneself if one is to seize on the Living God: 'The soul can only seize on him by going beyond itself'.[45]

Such distinctions are perhaps superfluous for our purpose. What mainly concerns us is to know how to arrive at making the sweet discovery of God within us. The first step is: to return into yourself, to return to your heart. ('Heart' and 'inner self' in biblical language mean that which is said of the depths of the soul.) 'Return to the heart,' St Augustine exhorts us.

> You are wandering outside, an exile from yourself! You do not recognize yourself and ask by whom you were made. Return to the heart. There examine what perhaps you perceive about God, for the image of God is there. Truth dwells in the inner self.[46]

All this implies specific choices. First, the habit of recollection. We live in a civilization entirely directed outwards. We send our space-probes to the very edge of the solar system but we do not know about 'probing' the heart. We move more comfortably in the macrocosm than in the microcosm which is ourselves. We favour escapism rather than recollection. Escapism, getting out of oneself, is you might say the order of the day. Some folk there are of course who dream about solitude, but they only dream about it. They love it, provided it stays a dream and is never translated into the harsh reality this implies. Many people are frightened of silence. The human race is sick with noise. When what we really need are moments of silence and solitude, to be able to squeeze into those depths of the heart where Truth resides. 'God', writes a monk,

> has created you a silent soul. In baptism, in an inviolate silence, he filled it with himself – himself alone. Afterwards,

little by little, the world burst in. A babel of voices invaded it,
drowning out God's sweet voice, and ever since then uproar
reigns in it. Brothers and sisters, return to baptismal silence!
Three things produce this racket: memories, curiosity and
worries. Do not let them act.[47]

A water-mirror reflects the image of the person leaning over it,
but only if the water is perfectly still. If the water is rough or its
surface covered in ripples, it won't reflect anything at all, you
won't be able to see the bottom any more and everything will
look murky. Useless anxieties, unwarranted haste, likewise make
our souls unable to reflect the image of God. Divided and scat-
tered, like a looking-glass smashed to a thousand fragments.
Even so, it is not enough just to be calm. The calm must be inhab-
ited by thought about God, not about ourselves. When I think
about myself, my own deformed image displaces the image of
God in the mirror of the soul and wipes it out.

   We must not let ourselves be misled by people who say that
God is to be encountered outside us: in contemplation of the
world, in our brothers and sisters, in the struggle for justice. All
true – but how can you discover God in these various realities, if
not through your own heart?

With St Augustine, let us pray to be granted the knowledge of
how to go back into ourselves:

> O God, from whom to turn away is to fall,
> to whom to turn is to rise again,
> in whom to abide is to stand firm . . .
> God whom no one loses unless deceived,
> whom no one seeks unless already called,
> whom no one finds who is not purified . . .
> Grant I may know myself and may know you.[48]

9 Who are you, Lord, and who am I?

The last words of the prayer we have just said ('Grant I may know myself and know you') express an important truth: knowledge of God is also the way to achieve knowledge of self. Only by knowing God can self-knowledge be ours.

From antiquity onwards, the wise have laid the command on themselves, 'Know yourself' and employed every means available to reach that result. To the traditional methods of introspection, the modern age has added another all its own: depth psychology. But by these and other similar means, always only partial elements, aspects and states of mind are grasped. A general synthesis of the self perceived as person, as whole, is lacking. Hence true self-knowledge is also lacking, since 'only the whole is the truth'.

To reach this different kind of knowledge needs a background and a measure that can only be God. The philosopher Kierkegaard, whom we shall be meeting more than once in the course of our journey, says:

So much is said about human pain and poverty. I seek to understand them, I have also known various cases at first hand. So much is said about wasted lives. But only that man's life is wasted who has let it go by, beguiled by life's joys and worries, in such that he has never, by an eternal decision, become aware of himself as spirit, as 'I'; or in other words – which is the same thing – because he has never realized, because he has never, in the deepest sense, intuited that there is a God, and that he, he himself, his own self, stands in this God's presence . . . I feel as if I could weep for an eternity at the thought that poverty such as this can exist![49]

Only when we accept the Living God into our own lives do we become complete persons and thus come to self-knowledge. A herdsman, Kierkegaard goes on, may be a self only vis-à-vis his cows if, living with the cows all the time, he has only the cows against which to take his own measure. A king may be a self to his subjects and feel no end of a fellow. A child feels itself to be a 'self' in relation to its parents; a citizen, in relation to the State . . .

But what infinite reality does the 'self' not acquire in acquiring the knowledge of existing in God's presence, in becoming a human 'self' whose measure is God . . . But what an infinite accent falls upon the 'self' by having God as its measure!

There was a period, spanning the eighteenth and nineteenth centuries, when, the idea of a personal God and of a positive revelation having been pushed out of circulation, philosophers and poets chose to see the state, or nature, or the world, or the Spirit (this being understood as meaning the overall product of human freedom and its sphere of operation) as the ultimate context in which human beings exist and achieve self-knowledge.

The yardstick was lacking. In this situation, human beings became like certain impressive medieval cathedrals overlooking squares too narrow for them or where in the course of the centuries other buildings and hovels have been built into the shelter of their walls. One cannot get far enough away to take in an impression of the whole, and this may in turn produce an almost physical feeling of discomfort. One sees the detail but lacks a general view, which alone would allow us to admire the work in itself and in its setting.

The reason for this restricting of the human horizon isn't hard to find. It is as though, without admitting it even to themselves, people were trying to avoid any confrontation from which they couldn't be sure in advance of being able to emerge victorious. They knew they could emerge victorious from a confrontation with nature and the world, because

> even if the universe were to crush him, man would still be nobler than his killer. For he knows that he is dying and that the universe has the advantage over him; whereas the universe knows nothing of this.[50]

On the other hand, they knew very well they couldn't emerge victorious (in the sense in which they used the word) from the encounter with the Living God, and so they ruled out any such confrontation. But in so doing they renounced that 'authenticity' which they often proclaimed to be their supreme ideal. They renounced the possibility of knowing who they were. And stayed poor 'herdsmen'.

Religious people, however, and especially the saints, seek nothing other than this confrontation and value it above all else. They desire it, even though knowing they will emerge as though seared by this encounter: for it reveals not only one's 'being' to one, but also one's 'being a sinner'. St Francis of Assisi would

spend whole nights repeating: 'Who are you, O my most sweet
God? And who am I, your most vile servant?', now raising his
eyes to heaven, radiant with joy, now lowering them to the
ground, filled with confusion. In uttering these words, he was
given, he said, two lights: one of knowledge of himself, the other
of knowledge of the Creator.[51] These are the two types of knowledge that, for saints and sages, have always constituted the twin
peaks of true wisdom.

A modern who discovered God in his own soul and made of
the two realities – God and the soul – the poles between which his
entire quest was to unfold, was Cardinal Newman. His 'conversion', which occurred when he was fifteen, he describes as

> confirming me in my mistrust of the reality of material
> phenomena, and making me rest in the thought of two and
> two only absolute and luminously self-evident beings, myself
> and my Creator.

He goes on to say:

> If I am asked why I believe in God, I answer that it is because
> I believe in myself, for I find it impossible to believe in my
> own existence without believing also in the existence of Him
> who lives as a Personal, All-seeing, All-judging Being in my
> conscience. ... I know I am right. How do I know it? I know
> that I know![52]

This clearly is not a universally valid proof that God exists. It is a
testimony. But for our purpose, in this book, by now we know,
testimony is as good as proof, if not better. 'It is absolutely necessary,' to quote Kant again, 'to be convinced of God's existence,
but it is not so necessary to prove it.'[53]

During his journey home from Italy, Newman composed a famous verse-prayer, which we should at least in part now make our own, as we pray that we too may receive that light which was kindled in him at the age of fifteen, inspiring him jubilantly to exclaim: 'I and my Creator!':

> Lead, kindly Light, amid the encircling gloom,
> Lead thou me on;
> The night is dark, and I am far from home,
> Lead thou me on.
> Keep thou my feet; I do not ask to see
> The distant scene; one step enough for me.

Moses entered the cloud

We have been trying thus far to uncover the ways that lead to the knowledge of God, that is to say, where to seek him. But what does 'knowing' mean when we talk about God?

In the Book of Exodus we read: 'Moses approached the dark cloud where God was' (Exodus 20:21). And again, 'Moses went right into the cloud and climbed on up the mountain' (Exodus 24:18). In another Old Testament book we read of Moses that God 'led him into the darkness and gave him the commandments face to face' (Ecclesiasticus 45:5–6). These statements have always exercised a great fascination over the more attentive students of Holy Writ. In them they have seen that great principle expressed by which God reveals himself . . . by veiling himself. This veil, represented by the cloud in the Old Testament, in the New Testament becomes the very flesh of Christ. Christ enters the sanctuary 'through the veil (or curtain), that is to say, his flesh' (cf. Hebrews 10:20). God, who is light, reveals himself through darkness; he who is all majesty, reveals himself in humility. True it is, God reveals himself 'by his opposite'.

Here is one example of this mystical interpretation of the symbol of the cloud, which has exerted enormous influence on Western spirituality. 'Then Moses frees himself,' writes Dionysius the Areopagite,

> from the things that are beheld and from those that behold them, and plunges into the Darkness of Unknowing, wherein he renounces all the apprehensions of his understanding and is enwrapped in that which is wholly intangible and invisible, belonging wholly to Him that is beyond all things and to none other; and being through the passive stillness of all his reasoning powers united by his highest faculty to Him that is wholly Unknowable, of whom thus by a rejection of all knowledge he possesses a knowledge that exceeds his understanding.[54]

This is what, right away in the title of his book, the anonymous author of *The Cloud of Unknowing* also meant to tell us.

What should we conclude from this? That the highest part of the person, I mean the reason, is excluded from the search for God? That we are forced to a choice between following faith or following reason? This is what is usually thought, but it's a pretty facile conclusion. By entering the cloud, that is to say, by believing, a human being doesn't renounce his or her own rationality but transcends it – something very different. Having used up reason's resources, we allow it to perform the supreme act, for 'the last step reason can take is to recognize there is an infinity of things beyond it'.[55] The last words reason cries out to us before she falls dumb, if we question her about God, are the same ones as the rest of creation shouted earlier, when reason herself was going in search of God: 'Seek beyond me!'

Rightly regarded as one of the most strenuous defenders of the demands of reason, St Thomas Aquinas writes:

God as an unknown is said to be the terminus of our knowledge in the following respect: that the mind is found to be
most perfectly in possession of knowledge of God when it is
recognized that His essence is above everything that the
mind is capable of apprehending in this life.[56]

The moment reason recognizes her limitations, she shatters and
transcends them; she realizes she cannot understand, but also
understands that 'a God who is understood could no longer be
God'. By the working of reason this recognition is produced,
which is therefore an exquisitely rational act. It is, literally, a
'learned ignorance'.[57] An ignorance achieved by reason, by
knowing that we do not know.

So we should rather therefore say the opposite, that is, that
anyone not recognizing reason's capacity for self-transcendence
is imposing limitations on her and degrading her. 'Until now,'
writes Kierkegaard,

people have always said this: To say one can't understand
this or that doesn't satisfy science, which seeks to understand. – This is wrong. One ought to say precisely the opposite: should it happen that human science doesn't wish to
recognize there are things it cannot grasp or – even more
precisely – things which it clearly can 'grasp that it can't
grasp', then all is thrown into confusion. It is therefore the
task of human understanding to grasp that there are, and
what are, things it cannot understand.[58]

But what is the darkness made of, of which we have been
speaking? Of the cloud which at a certain point interposed itself
between the Egyptians and the Jews, it is said, according to one
possible reading of the biblical text, that 'it was dark on one side
and light on the other', or again, 'dark for one lot and light for

the others' (cf. Exodus 14:20). Another powerful symbol! The
world of faith is dark for those who look at it from outside, but
light for those who are inside. With a special light – of the heart
rather than of the mind. These are the famous 'reasons of the
heart that the reason doesn't understand'. In the *Dark Night* of St
John of the Cross (a variant on the theme of the cloud), the soul
declares it will follow its new road,

> without light or guide
> save that which burned in my heart . . .

A light, however, that is 'surer than the mid-day sun'.[59] Whoever
it was who said: 'We only see well with the heart', was right.

So there we are: what we have been saying is clear for some
and not for others. One cannot pretend to offer rational proof of
these things to people who are still 'outside'. The only way to
enter that new light is to take the plunge and say: 'I believe'. I
believe in order to understand; not the contrary, I believe because
I have understood. It's like those modern kind of doors which
open of their own accord once you set foot beyond a given point.

Speaking of the Mother of God, Blessed Angela of Foligno
says that she was

> so ineffably united to the supreme and absolutely ineffable
> Trinity that she enjoyed something in life of what the saints
> enjoy in the heavenly homeland: a joy of incomprehension,
> since they understand that they cannot understand.[60]

'The joy of not understanding!' In these words the saint has said
the loveliest and most important thing we need to know on this
whole theme of the unknowability of God; far from giving rise to
frustration, this unknowability is designed to fill us with enthu-
siasm and joy. So much so that at the end of our ascent, we should

be really disappointed if it proved not so and we found we could understand everything. To know that God is infinitely greater, lovelier, better than whatever we can manage to imagine, and that all this is for us, so that our joy may be complete; so that the thought may never so much as enter our heads that we might get bored in spending eternity with him!

Let us borrow this prayer by a lady who has preceded us to Sinai's peak:

> Give me, Lord, a simple, ignorant knowledge of yourself who are the cause of all things. Let all be dense cloud around me and may my soul hurtle forward through it towards the light and joy of your love.

11   I shall stand at my post

Precisely because God is by definition incomprehensible, the surest method of drawing near to him is that of always going beyond everything. Of transcending. We never halt at any goal we reach, but keep on murmuring the words: 'Yes, but this isn't God.' Following each positive statement with a negation. Going therefore beyond the cosmos, beyond the human soul, beyond the very letter of the Scriptures, which nevertheless have helped us up till now to have some inkling of the Living God.

God is reached by exclusion. *Ex-cludere* means 'to shut out', to leave aside. Bible and Christian spirituality offers us a whole series of examples showing how this method works in practical terms and how we can make use of it in our own lives.

Let us start with the story of Jacob: he wrestles with God and obtains God's blessing. What had happened before this mysterious encounter with God, which ended with the patriarch exclaiming: 'I have seen God face to face'? 'Jacob', it is written,

got up and, taking his two wives, his two slave-girls and his

eleven children, crossed the ford of the Jabbok. After he had
taken them across the stream, he sent all his possessions over
too. And Jacob was left alone (Genesis 32:22ff).

The Jabbok is a torrent that runs through a ravine. Between
himself and the rest of the world and his own family he puts a
torrent and a ravine (or at least a considerable distance) if we
interpret the text as meaning that he stayed behind, while sending
the rest of the caravan on ahead. All this took place in the deep
silence of the desert night.

The features characteristic of the method we have called
exclusion now begin to take shape before our eyes. Wives, slave-
girls, children, property, first everything must be sent away; we
have to say goodbye to everything. And hastily – as when we
expect the arrival of someone who, we know, will not come until
he is sure of finding us alone.

This biblical picture reminds us of another. Before receiving
his famous 'vision' to be inscribed on tablets and the great oracle
about the righteous 'who live by faith', the prophet Habakkuk
had said to himself (as though obeying an inner command):

> I shall stand at my post,
> I shall station myself on my watchtower,
> watching to see what he will say to me . . . (Habakkuk 2:1).

One day, this passage spoke to me in a very special way. I seemed
almost to see with my own eyes and myself want to do what the
prophet lets us glimpse. To climb up and up the narrow stairs of a
tower or castle, not speaking to anyone, leaving floor by floor,
people, noises, everything behind: not stopping till I reach my
station on the watchtower, there where there is nothing before
me except the sky to gaze at and God to talk to, and everything
else down there below my feet. This is of course an image of

another ascent, by stairs that lead at the top to an absolutely interior castle. For a long time re-reading or listening to the prophet's words and reliving that state of mind were one and the same thing. I only had to say to myself: 'To the ramparts!' Each time, the image acted as a potent help to prayer, releasing me from all that would hold me back.

In the Gospel too, Jesus gives us one of these image-guides. 'When you pray,' he says, 'go to your private room, shut yourself in and pray to your Father in that secret place' (Matthew 6:6). Jacob put a torrent between himself and the rest of the world. Habakkuk had in mind to put a fortress. Jesus suggests we put a closed door. The anonymous medieval author whom we have already mentioned suggests we put a cloud and calls it the cloud of forgetfulness:

> As the cloud of unknowing is above you, between you and your God, in right so manner put a cloud of forgetting beneath you, between yourself and all the creatures that ever be made.[61]

The monks of old, not content with these barriers as being too easily overcome, thought good to put the desert between themselves and the world. But we shouldn't allow ourselves to be misled on their account. The words 'flee, be silent' (*fuge, quiesce*) which they were for ever repeating to themselves and their disciples, as also the idea of *fuga mundi* derived from this, is not a flight *from* something (this being merely secondary and the means) but a flight *towards* something. It is a flight, and that a dizzying one, towards the Living God.

On this topic, however, the most affecting story is that in which the main roles are filled by Augustine and his mother Monica at Ostia in the course of their journey back to Africa. Let us listen to the salient passages of Augustine's account of that sacred hour. (The introductory words will help us make a mental picture of the scene.)

> The day was approaching on which my mother was to leave this life and it so happened that she and I were standing alone, leaning in a window which looked onto the garden of the house where we were staying, at Ostia on the Tiber. There we were, far from the noise of the crowds, and after our long and weary journey were resting before our sea voyage. So we were alone and talking together very sweetly ... Then, with our affections burning still more strongly towards the Selfsame Being, we raised ourselves higher and step by step passed over all material things and even heaven itself. And still we went upward, meditating and speaking and looking with wonder at your works and we came to our own souls, and even went beyond them to reach that region of never-failing plenty. And as we talked, yearning for it, we did with the whole strength of our hearts' impulse just lightly come into touch with it and we sighed and we left bound there the first-fruits of the spirit, to return to the empty sound of our own mouths ... On the day when this happened, this world with all its delights seemed worthless to our eyes.[62]

So, here we have a few cases of people who have actually 'encountered' the Living God. Keeping their stories 'as living ikons before our mind's eye', let us try, as far as we may, to imitate them. St Anselm exhorts us to do so, in words echoing Augustine's story:

> Come now, insignificant wretch, leave your preoccupations behind for a time, seclude yourself for a while from your disquieting thoughts. Turn aside now from heavy cares and

> disregard your wearisome tasks. Attend for a while to God
> and rest in him. Enter the inner chamber of your mind; shut
> out all else except God and whatever is of aid to you in
> seeking him; after closing the chamber door, think upon your
> God. Speak now, my whole heart, speak now to God: I seek
> your face, your face, O Lord, I seek . . . Teach my heart where
> and how to seek you, and where and how to find you.[63]

How 'spiritual contact' with the Living God occurs is ever a
mystery, something new and unpredictable. Two things however
always precede and accompany that moment, like two silent
handmaids who exchange their respective mistresses' messages:
grace and freedom. 'God', writes a great mystic,

> is like a sea, rising and falling. Unceasingly he extends his
> flow to all who love him and, at his ebb, draws back to him
> all those whom he has filled.[64]

These words summon up a picture before the mind's eye: of the
sea which, rising at high tide, invades the shore, and at its ebbing
draws everything away with it that it finds free. But some little
boats are made fast fore and aft to a cradle or moored by a rope
to a post driven into the ground. The sea surrounds and caresses
them as though inviting them to follow it. For a while they allow
themselves to be lifted, and float but, being tied up as they are, do
not follow the sea as it ebbs; they stay beached, while the other
boats which were free float away on the calm and sunlit sea.

So it befalls with God. He sends his word and his grace as a
kindly flood to envelop the soul and invite it to follow him in his
immensity. Some souls are 'detached', are ready, and joyfully
follow him; they willingly let themselves be 'swallowed up' by
him; others are tied by the ropes of ingrained habits or fear of the
unknown. For a moment or two they allow themselves to be

lifted and rocked to and fro, but when it's a matter of taking the decision to cast away, they don't feel so inclined and stay ashore. Which shall we be? One day shall we know the rapture of the open sea, or shall we be like those little boats stuck on the beach, rotting away in the salt sea air?

There is a poem by Tagore which might have been written precisely to arouse our desire to cast off our moorings and once again find ourselves 'to you through you' with God, far from all else. In it, addressing God, the poet says what we may now repeat as a prayer, to remind God and ourselves of a promise:

> At break of day
> it was whispered we had sailed
> away in a boat, you and I,
> and no one else in the world had known
> about this our pilgrimage . . .
>
> In that ocean without shore,
> to your absorbed and silent smile,
> my songs will burst forth
> in melodies free as the waves,
> free from the slavery of words . . .[65]

12 Blessed are the pure in heart for they shall see God

So there are various things that need to be 'excluded', for us to be able to draw near to God: noise, the crowd, the world, creatures, self. But there is one thing it is absolutely – not relatively – necessary to exclude. One thing of which it is written that 'it digs a gulf between us and God' and forces him 'to hide his face' (Isaiah 59:2). Sin!

Scripture says that to run towards God we must 'throw away everything that weighs us down and the sin that clings so closely' (Hebrews 12:1). (The word translated as weigh down, *oncos*, is the same as gives us the term oncology and means tumour; clinging so closely suggests a soft but stifling embrace.) To pretend you can draw near to God without drawing away from sin is like believing you can walk forwards and backwards at the same time. For sin, according to the most classic of definitions, is a 'turning away from God' (*aversio a Deo*) in order to turn back to creatures.

The real obstacle to knowledge of God is not usually of an intellectual but of a moral nature; it is more often sited in the will than in the intellect. 'You say to me, "Show me the God you

have!"' exclaims a Christian apologist of long ago, addressing
the pagans of his day, 'and I reply, "Show me the man you are!"'[66]
And he goes on to explain what he means. God can only be seen
by those who have healthy spiritual eyes. The sun may shine as
brightly as you please, but if you are blind you will see nothing;
you will say the sun doesn't exist. Again: if a mirror is covered in
rust, it won't reflect the face of anyone looking into it any more.
By the same token a person obscured by sin cannot see God, since
sin spreads dimness and darkness in the heart.

Pascal made an observation with regard to the so-called
'libertines' of his day – not to be taken as absolute (for there are
morally unexceptionable people among the atheists, just as there
are libertines among believers!) but still containing a strong
element of truth: '"I would soon have renounced pleasure," says
the libertine, "if I had faith." But I reply, "You would soon have
had faith if you had renounced pleasure."'[67] It is not within a
believer's power to give faith and so test the truth of the libertine's
claim; but it is in the libertine's power to renounce sin and so find
out if what the believer says is true.

To the question: 'Who shall ascend the mountain of the
Lord?', the psalmist immediately replies: 'He who is clean of
hands and pure of heart' (Psalm 24:3–4). Jesus condenses all
biblical teaching on this subject into one short sentence: 'Blessed
are the pure in heart: for they shall see God' (Matthew 5:8).

We know that, in the Bible, as for that matter in common
speech, pure and purity have a huge range of meanings. There is
aesthetic purity, purity of line, and a moral purity that in its turn
expresses itself in our thoughts and intentions, and hence in our
lives. It is also common knowledge that it primarily means a
certain type of behaviour in the sexual sphere which is marked by
respect for its intrinsic end and for the will of the Creator. We
cannot enter into contact with God, who is spirit, other than
through our own spirit. But disorder or (worse still) aberrations in

this area have the effect – and this is acknowledged by everybody, not only by moralists – of clouding the mind. It is like kicking your feet in a pond: mud rises from the bottom and makes the water murky. God is light, and people of this sort 'hate the light'.

Sin does not allow us to see the face of God, or if it does it shows it thoroughly deformed. It makes him not the friend, the ally and father, but the foe. The enemy who bars the way to your wicked desires with his 'Thou shalt' and 'Thou shalt not'. In the human heart, sin gives rise to a veiled rancour against God, to such an extent that if it depended on the sinner, he could sometimes wish God didn't exist at all.

As a rule we urge people to flee from sin for negative reasons: because it debases the creature, because it leads to death and perdition. We overlook the stronger, the positive reason: they who renounce sin find God! They find what in sin they sought in vain. It was the thought of 'bread and to spare' in his father's house that made the prodigal son decide to give up the pigs' acorns – not their bitter taste. Perhaps more could be achieved with the corrupt society of today by telling it about the Living God, by making him shine forth in all his beauty before its eyes, by arousing a yearning for him, rather than by throwing its sins in its face.

This approach is not directed only to 'libertines' and unbelievers, but also – and perhaps primarily – to us who profess to be believers and are called to proclaim the Living God to others into the bargain. When God called the prophet Isaiah, he didn't give him instructions about what to say and how to speak about him; he simply touched his mouth with a red-hot coal, saying: 'Your guilt has been removed and your sin forgiven.' In that same instant, the prophet felt a new and irresistible need come to birth in his heart, to proclaim the thrice-holy God, which made him cry out: 'Here I am, send me!' (cf. Isaiah 6:1–8).

We must have definitively 'broken with sin' (cf. 1 Peter 4:1) to experience our joyful ability to proclaim the mystery of God.

Then our voice acquires a new, free tone, one different from before: no longer merely apologetic, but kerygmatic. Even if it is not in fact possible to *prove* the existence of God, it is certainly possible to *show* it! A priest and a lady were once sitting opposite one another in the train. The priest was coming back from a course of spiritual exercises. He had just received absolution, was happy at having had his sins forgiven. Silence reigned, but at a given moment the lady lowered the book she had been reading and, leaning towards the priest, exclaimed: 'Father, your face makes me believe in God!'

What an incentive we have decisively to resume our struggle against sin, if need be 'to the point of bloodshed'! (Hebrews 12:4).

> By being purified from shame, the stain incurred through wickedness, and by returning to our natural beauty, we can approach the Paraclete. And he, like the sun, when your sight is purged, will show you in himself the image of the Invisible. And in the blessed vision of the image you will see the ineffable beauty of the Archetype . . . And as clear, transparent bodies, if a ray of light fall upon them, become radiant themselves and diffuse their splendour around, so souls illuminated by the indwelling Spirit are rendered spiritual themselves and impart their grace to others.[68]

In the words of the *Miserere* let us pray to be granted a 'pure heart' that 'sees' God:

> Wipe away all my guilt.
> God, create in me a pure heart . . .
> I shall teach the wicked your paths,
> and sinners will return to you.
> Lord, open my lips,
> and my mouth will proclaim your praise.

13 Go out and stand
in the presence of the Lord

The time has now come to listen at greater length to the voices of
some of the great veterans of Mount Sinai. The first of these are
the prophets.

The task *par excellence* of the prophets was to help the
Israelites to live in the presence of God. This didn't isolate them
from or make them heedless of the people's material or social and
political needs. Only it prompted them to confront each new situation with God as their starting point. Elijah was one of those
fiery prophets who forced everyone, even kings, to stand
constantly under the judgment of God. But to be able to
discharge this task, Elijah first had himself to be converted and
learn 'to stand in the presence of the Lord'. Let us briefly remind
ourselves of his experience, also because it can help us to grasp
what is awaiting us if we too wish, in our small way, to be
witnesses to the Living God.

Elijah is the man who finds himself in the centre of a deadly
confrontation between the holiness of God and the sinfulness of
the people. After innumerable gruelling encounters with the

ruling powers at the head of Israelite rebellion, one day he suffers
a crisis of exhaustion and discouragement. 'I am the only one
left,' he bitterly complains (1 Kings 19:10). He experienced the
temptation to run away, to give up, thinking to take refuge in the
solitude of the desert: 'Elijah was afraid and fled for his life'
(cf. 1 Kings 19:3ff). When his dejection was at its worst, he sat
down under a furze bush and exclaimed: 'Lord, I have had
enough. Take my life.' He was willing to let himself die.

But see how the encounter with the Living God transforms
this moment of crisis, from the experience of flight and discouragement into one of recovery and victory. An angel shows him
a loaf cooked on the embers and says to him: 'Get up and eat,
or the journey will be too long for you.' With the strength given
him by this food, he walks forty days and forty nights until
he reaches the mountain of God, Horeb, that is to say Mount
Sinai.

Even so, the crisis has not been resolved. Having reached
Horeb, Elijah, we read, 'went into a cave to spend the night in it'.
Possibly he had a period of rest and quiet in mind, a little relaxation. Having seen the apparent futility of his efforts, the prophet
entered a state of passive waiting, almost one of apathy. 'When
the Lord makes himself heard again,' he thought, 'I'll get up, I'll
go to work . . .' Someone has described this state of mind, which
is not infrequent among God's servants:

When our soul begins no more to desire the beauties of
the earth, most times a sluggish spirit furtively worms its
way into it, not allowing us willingly to serve at the ministry
of the word, nor leaving us a firm desire for future blessings,
yet making us think this temporal life utterly contemptible
. . . We can however flee this luke-warm passion begotten
of sluggishness, if we fix our mind between very restricted
limits, turning our gaze exclusively on recollection of God.

For only thus, by resuming the race towards its Saviour, can
the intellect draw back from this sort of irrational wastage. [69]

The Lord didn't leave his prophet in that state for long: 'What are
you doing here, Elijah? Go and stand on the mountain in the
presence of the Lord.' What does this mean? That relaxation of
effort is not allowed, that there are no slack times with God. The
dark night of the spirit can't be spent in shelter, sleeping, but in
watching, waiting 'ready with one's belt tightened, lanterns
burning, like those who are waiting for the master, to open the
door to him the moment he knocks' (cf. Luke 12:35ff). We have
to stand ever on the sill of our own nothingness and our own
powerlessness, but actively, not passively and inertly. Stretching
out towards the One who has disappeared but who will return.

Elijah's case also tells us of the importance of silence in these
situations. He had to let the voices and noises outside and within
him die away, turn his back on every other presence, including
that of 'his boy', to enter 'the presence of the Lord'. In Elijah's
lonely wait on the mountainside, as in that of any other prophet,
there are first hurricane, fire and earthquake: that is to say, every
kind of ordeal, of worry and fear, making God's absence felt all
the more acutely ('But the Lord was not there in the wind, in the
fire, in the earthquake . . .') At last however, heralded by the
murmur of a gentle breeze, that is to say, by peace of heart, see,
God returns and, with him, the courage and joy to begin again.
The encounter with the Living God takes place at the end of a
road of purification, of emptying and annihilation of self. 'No
one can see God and survive,' the Bible says. First we have to die.
A woman of our day who has really stood on Sinai spiritually and
physically has written in connection with what took place before
her journey:

An encounter with God is always preceded by dark times of

doubt which black us out, so that his light can break in
without being mixed with the light of our misleading reason.[70]

Scripture itself has revealed how God forms his prophets and
witnesses:

> He takes him first through winding ways,
> bringing fear and faintness on him,
> trying him out with his discipline
> until he can trust him
> and testing him with his ordeals,
> but then comes back to him on the straight road
> and reveals his secrets to him (Ecclesiasticus 4:17–18).

What happens to Elijah is repeated in a very similar form in the
life of another great prophet, Jeremiah, he too being caught in the
midst of the deadly encounter between God's holiness and the
people's rebelliousness. One day, worn out, Jeremiah exclaimed:
'A disaster for me, mother, that you bore me!' (cf. Jeremiah
15:10ff). Temptation in his case took the form of a lament over
God's treatment of him: 'Haven't I genuinely done my best to
serve you? But, for me, you are a deceptive stream with uncertain
waters.' As much as to say: So wasn't it my bad luck to have
known you and been chosen by you? For Jeremiah, this too was
the occasion of a new conversion and an experience of the Living
God which was much deeper than what had occurred at his first
call. To the prophet's cry of 'Enough!' God replies, not by
reducing his demands but by increasing them. And the prophet
himself tells us: 'The Lord replied: "If you repent, I shall restore
you to plead before me. If you distinguish between the precious
and the base, you shall be as my own mouth."' As much as to say:
if you can tell the difference between what is valuable in the
prophetic life – to wit suffering – and what is not so valuable – i.e.

applause and success – then you shall be as my own mouth. How staggering: for God to regard Jeremiah as his own mouth!

All the same, a change of heart is required of the prophet: he must give up his attitude of self-pity and covert rebelliousness. He must abandon all his arguments, however plausible and true they may be, with a view to a purer, more detached faith. The prophet thus experiences in himself the judgment of God which he will have to proclaim to others. He experiences what it means 'to stand in the presence of the Lord of Hosts' and 'to dwell close to a devouring fire' (cf. Isaiah 33:14).

A modern writer puts words into the mouth of St Francis of Assisi, which to some degree evoke this same image of God for us. Dangerous to regard this as absolute; nonetheless it contains an element of truth we should be wrong to overlook.

'Up till now,' the Poor Man of Assisi said one day to Brother Leo, 'people have enumerated many terms of praise for the Lord. But I shall enumerate still more. Listen to what I shall call him: the Bottomless Abyss, the Insatiable, the Merciless, the Indefatigable, the Unsatisfied, He who has never once said to poor, unfortunate mankind: "Enough!" . . . If you ask, Brother Leo, what God commands without respite, I can tell you, for I learned it these past three days and nights in the cave: "Not enough! Not enough!"'

'I became angry,' Brother Leo goes on with his story. 'I felt overwhelming compassion for Francis.

'"What more can God expect of you? Didn't you restore San Damiano's?"

'"Not enough."

'"Didn't you abandon your father and mother?"

'"Not enough."

'"Didn't you kiss the leper?"

'"Not enough!"'[71]

Thus far the modern author. Perhaps Francis himself would have reminded us of another truth next door to this one: that even the incessant 'Not enough!' of God is love and grace, and that he not only puts it to effect in asking but, even before, in giving.

So let us pray as the Poor Man of Assisi used to pray in his *Praises for Each Hour*:

> Almighty, most holy,
> most high and sovereign God,
> the Sovereign Good, everything good, wholly good,
> who alone are good:
> to you let us render all praise, all glory,
> all thanks, all honour, all blessing
> and whatever is good. Amen! So be it!

14   I want God!

After the prophets, let us now question another class of veterans of Mount Sinai: the mystics. Mystics are people who have 'suffered God'.[72] Oh how painless this definition sounds when read in books and how terrible it actually is! Someone who long ago experienced this gave vent to this complaint: 'All your waves and breakers have rolled over me' and 'your terrors have annihilated me' (Psalms 42:7; 88:16).

There is a certain affinity between the way God made heaven and earth in the beginning and the way in which he makes saints today. For the saint and particularly the mystic has to go through the painful phase of chaos to be able to become 'cosmos', the new creation in which all is order, harmony and perfection. The dark night of the spirit has much in common with the 'formless void and darkness' of which the Book of Genesis speaks (Genesis 1:2). Evil and good, virtues and vices seem all mixed up in a whirl of thoughts and temptations which neither the mind can grasp, nor the will control. 'Then,' writes one mystic

we find ourselves forsaken in such manner as no longer to
have any knowledge of God, and fall into such distress as no
longer to know whether we have ever stood in the right way,
nor do we know any more whether God exists or not, or
whether we ourselves are alive or dead. And thus so strange a
pain falls on us, it seems to us the whole wide world is
weighing down on us. We no longer have any experience or
knowledge of God, yet everything else fills us with repug-
nance: so that we seem imprisoned between two walls.[73]

These men and women have 'risked their lives' in order to
approach God (cf. Jeremiah 30:21); they have wrestled with him
and, like Jacob, have emerged wounded for ever (cf. Genesis
32:23ff). When we read what they have written, or if we have the
luck to know one of them in the flesh while the terrible 'crossing'
is still in progress, how remote and even naive the shrewdest
arguments of atheists seem to be! Listening to what these atheists
say we get a feeling of astonishment or even of pain, as before
people speaking of matters manifestly unknown to them. Like
someone persuaded he is discovering endless grammatical
mistakes in what someone is saying to him and not realizing this
person is actually talking a different language which he doesn't
happen to know. But we feel no wish to set about refuting them,
for words actually said in God's defence at this moment seem
empty and out of place.

Mystics are the people *par excellence* who have discovered
that God 'exists'; also that he alone really exists and that he is
infinitely more real than what we normally call reality. They
know what it means 'to get back to things'.

It was precisely in one of these encounters that a female
disciple of the famous philosopher Husserl (he indeed who
launched the programme of 'getting back to things'), herself a
philosopher, Jewess and convinced atheist, one night discovered

the Living God. I'm talking about Edith Stein, who later became a Discalced Carmelite, was murdered by the Nazis in Auschwitz and has now been proclaimed Blessed by the Church. She was staying with some Christian friends of hers and one evening, when these had to go out, was left alone at home and, not knowing what to do, took a book at random from the shelves and began to read. It was St Teresa of Avila's autobiography. She read and read all night, unable to raise her eyes from the page. When she got to the end, she simply exclaimed: 'It's the truth!' Early that morning she went into town, bought a Catholic catechism and a pocket missal and, having studied them, went into a nearby church and asked the priest to baptize her.

For Christians at large, the mystics are like those explorers who first and covertly entered the Promised Land and then came back to report on what they had seen ('a land flowing with milk and honey'), urging the Israelites to invade it straightaway (cf. Numbers 14:6–9). Through their agency, the first flashes of eternal life reach us here below.

Unfortunately a certain literary fashion has succeeded in often neutralizing even this living 'proof' of God's existence, I mean the saints and especially the mystics. This has been achieved in a most remarkable way: not by reducing their number but by augmenting it, not by restricting the phenomenon but by extending it out of all proportion. I refer to authors and editors who, in a collection of mystics, in anthologies of their writings, or in histories of mysticism, put cheek by jowl, as though representing the same type of phenomena, St John of the Cross and Nostradamus, saints and eccentrics, Christian mysticism and medieval cabala, hermeticism, theosophy, types of pantheism and even alchemy. In my opinion, people who *a priori* deny the possibility and genuineness of mystical experience or who explain it away in terms of pathology, do less harm to genuine mysticism in comparison.

I shall not even pause over the position of those theological schools which – perhaps owing to the confusion I have just been pointing out – reject the idea of a Christian mysticism out of hand, or regard it as a pagan phenomenon, i.e. as the exaltation of the human. Such theses derive, they too, in great part from the fact that mysticism is being confused with the idea of mysticism. The mystics' experiences, viewed in concrete terms, biographically and not ideologically, are the strongest possible demonstration of the annihilation of the human, of one's own merits, virtues and pretensions to salvation. On the contrary, it is the experience that most displays God's absolute sovereignty of act and grace. True mystics are those who have once and for ever been 'converted' to the pure faith.

I have chosen one of these souls, whom we have already mentioned in passing, so as to hear her testimony in more detail. I mean Blessed Angela of Foligno. Already advancing in the ways of holiness, Angela one day made a bitter discovery: God was still not truly all to her. Her 'wanting God' was still 'wishful thinking', since the desire for him did not embrace her whole world and did not reach an absolute intensity. Then an extraordinary thing happened. She felt a new unity forming within her, as though her whole being were being concentrated into one point: body agreed with soul, intellect with will, and she became aware that she had only one wish henceforth. Whereupon the question was put to her soul: 'What do you want?' and the soul, crying out with all its might, replied: 'I want God!'

We spoke earlier of the 'judgments' as being an unmistakable feature of the Living God. It appears that in Angela's day the litanies of the saints, among other suffrages, also contained this one which ran: 'By all your holy judgments, deliver us, O Lord.' For she writes:

Nothing gives me such a complete knowledge of God as my

recognition of him through his judgments. At night or in the morning, when I recite a litany, praying to God as follows: 'Lord, deliver me by your coming, and deliver me by your nativity, and your passion,' there is nothing that delights me more than when I reach the invocation in which I proclaim joyfully and confidently: 'By your holy judgments deliver me, O Lord.' The reason is because I do not recognize God's goodness more than in one good and holy person, or even in many good and holy people, than in one or many who are damned ... Even if all the other truths of faith were shaken, I would still be sure of this one, namely, the justice of God's judgments. What depths are found there!

The confessor who collected and put these confidences of hers into writing makes the comment at this point: 'Here I realized she was saying the most marvellous things in the world.' But what exactly has the saint been saying? Nothing; that mere evocation of God's judgments had sufficed to convey a feeling of the holy Living God and pass this on to the listener. The latter had been seized with the sense of the 'numinous', the supernatural, as often happens today to people reading this mystic's words.

The saint was accustomed to say that souls who most felt God had least success in speaking about him, for the further they penetrated into knowledge of the infinite and indescribable God, the more their ability to speak of him diminished. Her same confessor begged her one day to explain matters more clearly, being convinced that with a little effort she could have done so. The saint replied by explaining what would happen to him if one day, having experienced God in that way, he were obliged to preach to the people. 'After climbing into the pulpit,' she told him,

you would stay silent for a moment, then addressing the people you would cry: 'Brothers, go away with God's

blessing, for I can tell you nothing about God today!' And in
silence you would come down from the pulpit.

Having for many years seen God 'in the midst of great darkness',
Angela was eventually transported by grace to the vision of God
'above the darkness'. Here we can only listen reverently to her
own words:

> Last Lent imperceptibly I found myself totally immersed in
> God even more profoundly than usual. Moreover, it seemed
> to me that I was in the midst of the Trinity . . . I am con-
> vinced that there is no saint, angel, or creature which has
> anywhere near the capacity to understand these divine work-
> ings and that extremely deep abyss . . . In this state, the soul
> is drawn out of all darkness and granted a greater awareness
> of God than I would have thought possible . . . Furthermore,
> I saw the One who is and how he is the being of all creatures.

Finally, one day, Angela arrives at the peak of peaks. She experiences what happens in the vision 'face to face', when all veils
drop that come between God and creature. 'Then,' she writes,

> my soul immediately presented itself before God with the
> utmost assurance and without any fear. This presentation
> was accompanied with greater delight than I have ever expe-
> rienced, with a new and most excellent joy, and with new
> miracles, so much so that I cannot imagine that my soul ever
> experienced anything so miraculous, so clear, and so new.
> Such was this encounter with God. In this encounter I simul-
> taneously perceived and experienced both that previous
> unspeakable manifestation of God to my soul, and this new
> manifestation of my soul and its presentation to God. In this
> I found new delights different from all previous delights, and

> I was told most high words which I do not want to be
> written.

As the day of her death drew near, Angela was heard to exclaim – by those who were around her – words that say more about the Living God than many a lecture: 'Oh, every creature is found wanting. Oh, the intelligence of the angels is not enough!' And to the question of those present: 'How are creatures found wanting and for what is the intelligence of the angels not enough?' she replied: 'To comprehend!'[74]

Endless books are written today, loaded with quotations from the philosophers, in answer to the question: 'Does God exist?' and often we get to the end of them with the question mark still not changed to an exclamation mark. And then, one day, we chance to open a little book like this, written by a certainly not learned woman in the Middle Ages, who had been a wife and mother, then a widow and lay Franciscan tertiary, and we suddenly discover that not only does God exist but that he is truly 'a devouring fire', 'sweetness without end'.

Let us pray and say with Jesus:

> I bless you, Father, Lord of heaven and earth, for hiding these
> things from the learned and the clever and revealing them to
> little children (Matthew 11:25).

15   I thank you,
Lord of the universe

In the analysis of the religious personality, we often witness the same basic procedure as is used in discussions about God. It is not concerned with the fact but with the idea. With stereotypes of religious personalities, not with people of flesh and blood, known, heard or at least read. The kind of person discussed or under scrutiny is not an historical figure, someone who has actually lived, but a laboratory product. Usually a caricature of a religious person, or else dealing with cases which religion itself recognizes as instances of pathological religiosity, of pseudo-religiousness.

The profane sciences now often become involved in the spheres of religion and faith, in exactly the way they reproach religion for having interfered in the sphere of science in time past. Their reproach is (and rightly) that, in evaluating the findings of science, religion didn't base itself on direct observation, on checks and experiments, but rather on preconceived notions of abstract and deductive type, or on the unquestioned authority of some great figure of the past, such as Aristotle. But this is exactly what a certain school of psychology does today when pontificating on matters of faith. It doesn't base itself on direct observation, doesn't judge religion from inside but from outside, not by what is known about it by direct experience but by what it observes at second hand, or basing itself on the authority and theories of some great name, such as Freud.

In a word, then, science treats religion today exactly as religion used at times to treat science in the past, as for instance in the case of Galileo. Today the experimental principle as criterion for determining the truth about a thing or a phenomenon applies to everything, except to religion. Also, it seems the precondition for saying something serious or 'scientific' about religion is *not* to have had any personal experience of it, to be immune to it and 'uncontaminated'. Exactly as with madness. Obviously the last people to have anything sensible or scientific to say about madness are the mad!

The Christian response to this challenge can only lie in a peremptory appeal to life, to real people, to the history of souls, and not to ideas. Often, without being aware of it, we fall into the error of accepting the ideological assumptions of non-believers: that one may manage to discover what religion or faith are by staying on the terrain of definitions and ideas, hence on the terrain of abstractions. The people who have struggled hardest against abstraction – to the point of making this their purpose in life and their claim to originality in their philosophizing – are the very ones who have constantly and systematically dealt in abstractions where religion is concerned. When it is a question of judging the authenticity or otherwise of the lives of people, I regard as abstraction all that is not a direct examination of the content or the unfolding of their lives, of their self-knowledge, of the impact they have had on their surroundings, of the final outcome of their lives, as also the quality and duration of time of the influence they exerted. Real and historical objectivity, in a word. This is the line to which we should hew. 'To one word', says one of the Desert Fathers, 'you may oppose another word; and to a doctrine another doctrine; but what can you oppose to a life?'

Another 'veteran of Mount Sinai' who helps us to measure the distance between the idea of a religious person (with which the fathers of atheism have laboured) and the actual religious person is St Simeon the New Theologian, whose life straddled the year 1000 and who is regarded as a model among the main representatives of Eastern spirituality, just as St Francis is for Western Christianity. (In this way we truly breathe the air of the Living God 'with both the Church's lungs', the Western and the Eastern.) Circumstances in life obliged St Simeon himself to describe his spiritual journey, and this makes his testimony particularly telling.

After a worldly life, he encountered God. The effect this encounter had on his life he describes in an impressive picture. Imagine, he says, a man struck down with poison in his bowels, tortured by an internal pain so strong as to make him forget all the external wounds he also carries on his body. If anyone curses and insults him, he doesn't react in anger, he allows anyone who wishes to rob him of his entire fortune. He is no longer in a state to care about anything or think about anything, since the distress he feels in his soul makes everything seem worthless. Every human being, righteous or unrighteous, and every creature existing under heaven seems to him blessed and worthy of esteem; he alone is unworthy to exist and breathe. Alone, cut off from all, seated as though on the dungheap of his many sins and wrapped in bottomless darkness and sorrow . . . This is the effect of awareness of sin; sin is the 'poison' eating away his insides.

This looks like good confirmation of the analysis of the religious character, as made by the atheistic philosopher: 'Where God is born, human nature dies.' But events do not stop here. That man – writes the saint, speaking of himself in the third person – in this his desperate state turns to God: 'Lord, see how low your handiwork has been brought . . . I have heard tell of you, I hardly know you and I tremble. What can I do? I have no excuses to offer you.' And now, slowly, slowly the bitterness starts to melt away and a new, unknown joy starts welling up like a sweet wine to replace the former poison. A joy so great that sometimes, when he is alone, he laughs at death, at hell, at all evil and all dangers. He feels a thousand times happier than if he were king of the whole world, than if he had unlimited wealth and health.

Then begins an intense effort at transformation, lasting for the rest of his life. Sometimes he is transported to heaven – whether in or out of the body not even he can say – but then once again he takes up his everyday life, as if nothing had happened, alarmed by his own misery. Sometimes he is in tears over the sufferings of others and his own. Until one day the moment comes for him to hear Christ's voice and find himself in his presence. 'O Master, and who am I? To what sweetness have you led me?' And the voice of the Spirit replies: 'Until you are delivered from the body, you will not be able to taste complete joy.' To which he responds: 'And how can it possibly be greater, more brilliant, than what I already have?' 'You are truly poor', comes the reply, 'if you are satisfied with these good things, for in comparison with the good things to come, these are like a paper drawing of heaven, as opposed to the real one.'

Having reached the end of his life, this man strikes up a ceaseless hymn of thanksgiving:

I thank you, I adore you, Lord of the universe, because you have glorified me, you have honoured me, you have overwhelmed me . . . You have caused me to pass from nothingness into being. You have given me freedom. You have purged my mind, you have expanded my vision . . .'[75]

The outcome of the encounter with God wasn't death, but new life at all levels, including that of the intellect. So full and fertile a life that generations and generations of Christians, especially in the East, have drawn and still draw on it today for all they are worth. An experience, hence, that has passed through that most exacting of sieves: that of time and cultural change and changing fashions. The result of this religious adventure was by no means impoverishment, no estrangement from life, no narrowing of horizons, but on the contrary the maximum expansion of the whole personality.

What is seen as fact in the lives of the saints only confirms what we have already read in Scripture. Commenting on the title 'God of Abraham, Isaac and Jacob', Jesus says, 'God is not the God of the dead but of the living, for to him everyone is alive' (Luke 20:38). The Living God is the condition why we too live. 'The glory of God', said St Irenaeus, 'is the living human being, but human life consists only in the vision of God.'[76] There is no rivalry or incompatibility between these two things, only a vital interdependence. The God of the Bible doesn't desire a human being's death, 'a bloody sacrifice', but that we should 'be converted and live' (Ezekiel 33:11). 'I have come', says Jesus, 'so that they may have life and have it to the full' (John 10:10).

At lives like those of Pascal and St Simeon, and of countless other believers from whose lips the cry 'Joy, joy, joy!' bursts forth, the unbeliever can muster but one defence: to throw suspicion on that joy. St Bernard says that once the choice has been made of total independence from God, people 'prefer to be independent of God even at the cost of being unhappy, rather than happy at the cost of being dependent on him'.[77] This is one aspect of the 'drama of atheist humanism': to be obliged to choose between happiness and freedom, to remain prisoners to a concept of freedom which of its nature leads to unhappiness.

Suspicion about mysticism has taken one very subtle and

insidious form. The mystical states as the mystics themselves describe them – it is argued – seem to have much in common with being in love; what mystics say about divine love is very similar to what occurs in human love. Won't their mystical marriage with God be a 'mystification' of ordinary marriage, a sublimation of it or substitute for it? I reply: Why not also consider the opposite hypothesis, to wit that ordinary marriage is the copy and the mystical one the real one? Isn't it more accurate in the sexual union to see a symbol, a parable and, as it were, a trial run for that other 'completeness' which the mystics have already tasted – all the more so since the former so evidently bears within itself the signs of incompleteness, of precariousness and of aspiration to something better and different? For the fact is, we haven't been created to live in an eternal relationship of couples, but in an eternal relationship with God, with the Absolute. It was no mystic, no churchman, who uttered the words: 'Everything transitory is but a parable'.[78]

The nature of this suspicion and its 'perversity' lies precisely in the fact that it shuns any confrontation and any possibility of being refuted. An argument or a fact can be refuted, but not a suspicion. Suspicion lies rather in the will than in the intellect. It has much in common with the nature of sin, in that it is 'voluntary'. The serpent didn't lead Adam and Eve to sin by producing an argument against God, but by throwing suspicion on him.

So suspicion can't be eliminated by reasoning. But perhaps it isn't even a good thing that it should be eliminated, for it is precisely this that makes believing the serious matter it is. It is precisely this possibility, outside and within us, that purifies faith and makes the believer humble. That is why none of the atheistic philosophers, so far mentioned or yet to be mentioned, has passed in vain across the face of the earth. Paradoxically, each has served and still serves the cause of the religion they thought they were destroying.

This is the prayer of the saint who has been our companion on this stage of our journey. Let us say it together:

> I thank you, I adore you, Lord of the universe,
> because you have glorified me,
> you have honoured me,
> you have overwhelmed me;
> you have caused me to pass from nothingness into being;
> you have given me freedom;
> you have purged my mind;
> you have expanded my vision.

16 A fiery torrent

With our recent thoughts about 'suspicion', at this point we have
entered a different climate. People who've been up the geograph-
ical Sinai tell of unexpected, violent storms of wind and rain, to
be encountered at certain stages on the climb. We too must now
go through one such storm and, as in similar cases, we shall
encounter people coming the other way and shouting: 'Go back,
go back!'

We have reached a critical problem. For we can't proceed
along our way as though the Living God were an uncontested
belief and one shared by everyone. As though this road towards
him were a quiet stroll or a triumphal march. Theoretical and
practical atheism exists. In real life we are constantly assailed by
voices contradicting those we have been listening to hitherto, and
these we cannot ignore. For two reasons: first, because we must
'always be ready, respectfully and courteously to give the reason
for our hope' (cf. 1 Peter 3:15); secondly, because the arguments
put forward by non-believers ultimately prove to be extraordi-
narily effective in purifying believers' faith in God.

In this context I shall have to touch on doctrines and philosophers not perhaps familiar to us all. But let no one be disheartened: very soon, you will see, we shall be back breathing calmer air. When one intends to cross a piece of water, the most important thing is not to stand on the beach and gaze at what may or may not be on the opposite shore, but to jump into a boat which will take you to that shore. The most important thing isn't to speculate about the Living God and digest everything philosophers have said for and against him, but to stand fast in the faith of the Church, and this will bring us to the Living God. Today too the challenge is hurled at believers: 'Where is your God?' (Psalm 42:3). And we must take up this painful challenge, even though knowing that the truth is reached by our cultivating, loving and presenting it for its own sake, rather than by polemics against our opponents.

In today's world, faith and proclamation of the Living God encounter so diffused and deep-rooted an obstruction as, in some cases, makes it impossible to begin, unless the obstacle is exposed and as far as possible removed. I mean a philosophy instilled into people's minds like some poison able to neutralize the Gospel tidings before they ever reach their heart. A kind of terrible 'contraception' killing the seed of the Word, preventing it from lodging in the mind and begetting eternal life in the soul. Even when it doesn't act as a counter-certainty to faith, it still acts as doubt, encouraging a suspension of judgment. I mean, an argument beguiling in its extreme simplicity, giving the impression of making everything clear at a stroke: 'God didn't make us in his image; we have made God in *our* image. When we worship God, we worship ourselves without realizing, and the more we worship God the more we worship ourselves.'

Here we have a sort of Copernican revolution in the spiritual field. If hitherto we have always thought of matter as a manifestation of the spirit, now it is proclaimed that spirit is derived from matter. It is the Platonic vision of the real, but stood on its head. No more is matter the projection, shadow and illusory image of the divine and spiritual world but, contrariwise, the divine world is now the projection and illusory image of human history and of nature.

Anyone with this presupposition who hears the Christian proclamation about God, about Jesus Christ and eternal life, will react exactly as we may imagine Copernicus and the few intimate friends to whom he had divulged his discovery would have reacted when, during a sermon or in conversation, they heard it said yet again that the sun goes round the earth: a wink as between folk who know how matters really stand, and everything returns to normal. The difference is that in the latter case they were right; but in this one they are wrong. The Copernicans of our day have gone beyond. They would have us believe that neither does the sun go round the earth, nor the earth go round the sun, but that the sun doesn't exist: it is only a projection of the earth's needs. 'No more heaven. No more hell. Just the earth, that's all.'[79]

The operation I am trying to describe is connected in particular with three big names in the culture of the last two centuries: Feuerbach, Marx and Freud. The last two built – the one declaredly, the other tacitly – on the theory of the first, which thus presents the original version. We know that for Feuerbach the divine essence was the human essence purified and liberated from the limitations of the individual, and contemplated and venerated as though it were an essence distinct in itself. 'In religion, man objectifies his own secret essence, reflecting himself in an entity which is his own deepest self.'

In other words, it isn't God who has created human beings in his own image and likeness as the Bible says, but we who have created God as a detached and fantastical image of ourselves. 'Faith in God is nothing other than faith in human dignity.' We attribute to God what is best in ourselves. So, the more perfection is conferred on God, the more is taken away from the human being; the more God is enriched, the more we are impoverished. 'Only a poor man has a rich God. God corresponds to the feeling of a need.'

In a second phase, Feuerbach was to make his teaching more specific, by identifying God with the essence of *nature*, rather than with the essence of humanity. 'Nature's existence does not depend on God's existence but, contrariwise, God's existence, or rather faith in his existence, is based on nature's existence.'[80] But basically this doesn't alter the situation.

It has always impressed me (and also made me somewhat suspicious) to note how some of the atheists' maxims are obtained by a systematic inverting of basic Christian truths. 'Jesus Christ,' says the Scripture, 'although he was rich, became poor for your sake, so that you should become rich through his poverty' (2 Corinthians 8:9). According to revelation therefore, God made himself poor to make us rich, not the other way round, as Feuerbach states here.

In German, the name Feuerbach means 'torrent of fire'. If you wish to arrive at the truth, Marx observes, you must forthwith pass through this fiery torrent.[81] It is 'the purgatory of modern thought'. It was indeed Karl Marx who gave this brilliant operation the success it has had, by making it the theoretical basis for his scientific atheism. But with a shift of emphasis. For Feuerbach, God is primarily the projection of the essence of humanity, of what humanity is, of its perfections, and only secondarily of its poverty and emptiness. God is therefore an illusion, but in his way a solid one, since rich in positive content. For Marx too, God is a projection, but rather than that of the positive essence of humanity, he is the projection of humanity's unsatisfied needs: not of what we are, therefore, but rather of what we lack, above all of our economic needs. 'Religion,' he writes,

is the moan of the oppressed, the soul of a heartless world
. . . It is the opiate of the people . . . Religion is nothing but an
illusory sun revolving round mankind until man finally
succeeds in revolving on himself.[82]

The stress shifts from the problem of God to that of the hereafter,
Paradise, that is to say. This is seen as the receptacle into which
humanity transfers its unfulfilled expectations and the 'tears'
shed in the valley of this life. The idea of God is born from the
idea of a hereafter, of an other-worldly reward. (The development of biblical religion gives the lie entirely to this thesis: for
Israel believed in an almighty and holy God centuries before
reaching certainty over the existence of an *other-worldly* recompense for the righteous, and went on believing in this kind of God
even after becoming certain about the non-existence, for them, of
an *earthly* recompense any different from or better than that
accorded to the wicked.)

God therefore is an illusory projection not of a human full-
ness but of a lack, a void. Hence a doubly negative one. God is
only 'the direction to which humanity hurls its cry'. With Freud,
the same theory assumes a new coloration, no longer socio-
economic but psychological, without however any change in
substance. Religion, God, is an 'illusion', the projection of the
unconscious need for fatherly and motherly protection which the
individual retains, having once left childhood. 'The roots of the
need for religion', writes Freud, 'are in the parental complex. The
almighty and just God is a grand sublimation of the father and
mother.'[83] Still therefore doubly negative: the projection is not of
a reality, but of a need, a void.

The influence these theses continue exerting on Western
people of average education is incalculable. And this is, generally
speaking, the idea of God and religion which is held as an uncontested assumption, as appears when the topic is discussed in the

so-called 'reviews of culture and current affairs', these being the most formidable of tools for spreading this type of secular culture. This is the suspicion which makes many believers hide their faith when they are out and about in the world.

Thus, in the world, the activity continues of him whom John Paul II in his encyclical on the Holy Spirit has called 'the perverse genius of suspicion'.[84] When we try to come to grips with and get to the heart of the arguments of the three authors mentioned above, we find that what is left behind isn't a proof that God doesn't exist, but merely a suspicion that he doesn't. For, even if the God in whom we believe were a projection of humanity, 'a desiderated essence', this would still not be saying anything about his existence or non-existence in reality. And this is not to take into account that the believer might with equal justification, in turn, throw suspicion on the non-believer on the grounds of Francis Bacon's observation that 'none deny that there is a God but those whom it maketh that there were no God'.[85]

Rather than on the divine, in this case suspicion fastens on the human. The human being it is who is now declared suspect in his deepest desires. Freud says:

> It would be very nice if there were a God who created the world and was a benevolent Providence, and if there were a moral order in the universe and an afterlife; but it is a very striking fact that all this is exactly as we are bound to wish it to be.[86]

A statement revealing a deep contempt for human nature. A thing becomes suspect by the very fact that we conceive of it and desire it! One might as well throw suspicion on love and marriage, since they correspond to a universal desire and deep need of the human heart, or deny that truth and happiness exist merely because human beings desire them. Here stands revealed what Henri de Lubac called 'the drama of atheist humanism'. Born to affirm human worth, modern atheism has ended up turning against human nature and becoming its negation.

It is therefore vital that we should, again and again, go back to the root and dismantle the brilliant but false operation giving rise to all this. But it is too the moment to imitate the way God acts, that is, to avoid condemning, together with their errors, their exponents and their consciences, which God alone knows. No crusade therefore, but rather respect for these people who, if nothing else, have consented to take the problem of God seriously. 'Of two beings who have no experience of God,' Simone Weil warns us, 'the one who denies him is possibly nearer to him.'

Reminding ourselves that, rather than a conquest, faith in the Living God is the gift of being sought by God, let us ask God for it, for ourselves and for others, in the prayer the Church offers 'for those who do not believe in God', during the Good Friday liturgy:

> Almighty and eternal God,
> you created mankind
> so that all might long to find you
> and have peace when you are found.
> Grant that, in spite of the hurtful things
> that stand in their way,
> they may all recognize in the lives of Christians
> the tokens of your love and mercy
> and gladly acknowledge you.

17   Our weapons for the battle

In discharging the task we have just set ourselves, St Paul's diagnosis at the beginning of the Letter to the Romans of the religious situation in the pagan world of his day will prove immensely helpful. A word, first of all, on the nature of this diagnosis and on its basis. It was easy to object to the Apostle: You are neither a philosopher nor have you made a thorough study of all the pagan authors, and yet in the course of one of your letters you claim to pass judgment on centuries of research and findings by people in comparison with whom you are nobody at all!

This was pretty much how – according to Origen – the pagan Celsus passed judgment on Holy Writ in his book against the Christians called *The True Account*. Naturally it is even easier today to level the same reproof against anyone trying, by means of St Paul, to refute centuries of brilliant European and Western speculation, names before whom – and very rightly – a whole culture and society bow down.

What did the Apostle reply to these predictable protests?

> The weapons with which we do battle are not carnal ones,
> but they have the power, in God's cause, to demolish
> fortresses. It is ideas that we demolish, every presumptuous
> notion that is set up against the knowledge of God (2
> Corinthians 10:4–5).

First of all then, our arguments are not 'carnal'. It isn't a question
of one rational opinion being advanced against another rational
opinion. They are not located on the same plane. This being so,
our approach will not be based on analysis and detailed refuta-
tion; instead we shall go straight to the nub of the problem.

Secondly, they have their power 'from God', not from
human beings, not from preachers. 'Not that we are so compe-
tent', says the Apostle

> that we can claim any credit for ourselves; all our compe-
> tence comes from God, who has made us the ministers of a
> new covenant, which is not of written letters, but of the
> Spirit (2 Corinthians 3:5–6).

Thirdly, they are able to demolish 'fortresses and presumptuous
notions'. With the theory we have mentioned we do indeed find
ourselves faced with a kind of presumptuous notion erected
against the knowledge of or the acknowledgment of God.
Human thought has, as it were, taken refuge behind these arguments. But the word of God, says Paul, has the power to
demolish these fortresses and destroy these reasonings. 'You
understand neither the Scriptures nor the power of God,' Jesus
used to say to his opponents (cf. Matthew 22:29), and the Spirit
today repeats these words to believers too: You do not know
the Scriptures and the power of God contained in them! Since
you have so little recourse to them, you expect just as little from
them! You base your message 'on persuasive philosophical

argument', rather than 'on the manifestation of the Spirit and of his power' (cf. 1 Corinthians 2:4). You think you have achieved the maximum when you think you have found a philosopher you can rely on to fend off another philosopher who is hostile to you; when you find a school that seems more favourable to you, as against a school which is opposed to you. Exactly as used to happen with the alternating alliances – now with Egypt against Syria, now with Syria against Egypt – which used so to provoke God and the prophets in the Old Testament without producing any true and enduring result. There is room of course among Christians for this type of effort called apologetics, but it is far from everything and by no means essential. The apostles didn't convert the world by apologetics but by proclaiming the kerygma in Spirit and in power.

Only this proclamation 'in Spirit and in power' must be radically humble too, free of any claim to 'conquer in time', that is to say, to carry off the victory on the human and rational plane as well. We often have to get the worst of the battle, so that God can emerge victorious. St Paul leaving the Areopagus in Athens with the audience exchanging pitying glances behind his back is an accurate enough image of what the proclaimer of the Gospel will encounter when he or she penetrates the citadel of this world's wisdom. Perhaps it was this very experience which prompted the Apostle later to write his words about the 'non carnal' weapons in our warfare.

As Origen prepared to reply to Celsus's criticisms of the Christian faith, he addressed a prayer to God, which I make bold at this point to adopt for myself:

> God grant that I may not come to this task with a mind and reason merely human and without any divine inspiration, so that those whom I am hoping to help may not put their faith

in human reason, so that every presumptuous notion that sets itself up against the knowledge of God may be destroyed. May he who gives 'the word to those who preach with great power' grant this also to me, so that by the word and power of God faith may spring up in those who read these words.[87]

18 Knowing God
is to acknowledge him

Now, at the beginning of St Paul's Letter to the Romans we read these words:

> The retribution of God from heaven is being revealed against the ungodliness and injustice of human beings who in their injustice hold back the truth. For what can be known about God is perfectly plain to them, since God has made it plain to them: ever since the creation of the world, the invisible existence of God and his everlasting power have been clearly seen by the mind's understanding of created things. And so these people have no excuse: they knew God and yet they did not honour him as God or give thanks to him, but their arguments became futile and their uncomprehending minds were darkened (Romans 1:18–21).

In the minds of people who have studied theology, these words are almost exclusively linked to the thesis that the existence of God can be known from the natural world. So, once this particular problem has been settled or has ceased to be of topical concern, they are rarely remembered and turned to account. Yet the problem of whether or not God can be known from nature is, in the context, quite marginal. The Apostle's words have something quite other to tell us; they contain one of those 'thunderclaps of God' which can shatter even the cedars of Lebanon.

The Apostle is intent on demonstrating something very precise: that all have sinned, without exception. In this respect, he divides the world into two parts: Greeks and Jews, that is to say, pagans and believers, and begins his indictment with the sin of the pagans. He locates the basic sin of the pagan world in its impiety and injustice. He says that this is an attack on the truth. Not on this or that truth, but on the fountainhead of all truths. And he forthwith explains what this involves. (This is where he touches just incidentally on the problem of God's knowability from nature.) The pagans, he says, can know God and indeed have known him; have known more or less clearly that there is a God. But they haven't given him glory and haven't given him thanks, as is due to God. They have halted halfway; they haven't drawn the ultimate conclusions. At a given point they have refused to pursue their arguments, and their minds have become darkened. This then is the sin that makes them 'inexcusable'.

So sin is not simple ignorance, as Socrates and the Greeks thought. It is not primarily to do with cognition, but with the will. Sin lies in the will's refusal to implement what is known to be true. It lies in refusing to see, not in simply not-seeing. In this, St John is in perfect agreement with St Paul. Sin lies in not accepting the light, and not accepting it rather than renounce one's own wicked works (cf. John 3:19). Sin isn't being blind, but seeing and not doing what we have seen (cf. John 9:41).

At this point however an objection arises. Why does the Apostle say here that the pagans 'have known God', when elsewhere he says the opposite, i.e. that 'the world was unable to recognize God through wisdom' (1 Corinthians 1:21)? The answer is that there are two modes of knowing: a Greek mode which we might call classical and philosophic, and a biblical mode. The modes have been authoritatively described as follows. For the Greek, knowing is similar to seeing, to gazing at an object, motionless, at a distance. From the object, the Greek seeks to extract its form, that is to say, its essential qualities, and by seizing on these to master the reality of the object itself. The known and the knowing remain separate; there is no interaction between them; for this would otherwise disturb the objectivity of the knowledge. For the biblical character, contrariwise, knowing means experiencing the object, entering into relationship with it. Knowing something means being interested in it, being involved with it. To sum up then, for the Greek, knowing God means contemplating the ultimate reality, Being in its changeless essence; for the Jew it means acknowledging God in his works and obeying his commands. The first mode is simple knowledge of God, the second is ac-knowledge-ment as well.

What the Apostle means to say is that the pagans have known God in the first mode, but haven't known him in the second. Knowing God doesn't in fact mean knowing all sorts of things about him, but it does mean knowing that he is God, that's all: '. . . so that you may know me and know that I AM,' God himself says (Isaiah 43:10). What is lacking and where the pagans' sin lies, is in not having given glory and thanks to God. Two things, we might say, are missing: recognition and gratitude.

The pagan philosophers, as St Augustine saw very clearly, were basically lacking in humility. That's why they couldn't accept the Incarnation and regarded it as preposterous and absurd. Symptomatic of this: humility never had a place in the list of Greek and pagan virtues. For them it always had a negative value: cowardice, insignificance, nothing more. So the idea that God himself could be humble struck them as the height of folly.

'Humility worries pagans.'[88] Paganism ends in immorality; it begins with lack of humility.

But what does this mean? In pagan literature were there perhaps no hymns of praise to the Godhead or thanksgiving for his benefits? No, Paul himself admitted that the Athenians were very respectful to the Godhead (cf. Acts 17:22). He has something more radical in mind. They have not given that glory and thanks which are rightly God's, and due only to him. Paul makes this very clear in the passage concerned: they have not given glory and thanks 'as to God', that is to say, as is due to God alone.

In pagan religion, fear and veneration were generally directed to the 'divine', which embraced either the divine in its positive aspect of God, or in its negative aspect of the demonic; the worship either of the celestial or of the infernal gods. When in the episode of our Lord's temptation, the devil asks Jesus to worship him, he isn't asking for anything new but for something he was accustomed to receive up till then from the pagans. Jesus it is who puts an end for ever to the ambiguity, by proclaiming, then and there, that one must worship the Lord God and 'him alone must one serve' (Matthew 4:10).

Thus, the pagan world lacked that radical perception that God is all, and that nothing and no one has the right to exist before him except by his favour. That we exist for God's glory, not for ours. That God is not something to be talked about and treated as we please, as if we could stand on equal terms with him and be of those entitled to converse with him. The sense of the qualitative difference between the divine and the human has disappeared, or perhaps – to be more accurate – has never existed, the radical difference between God and the individual being mitigated by a whole hierarchy of inferior beings appropriately called 'intermediate' divinities or those 'of second rank'.

The pagan consequently doesn't understand about an act which should be exclusively reserved for God; doesn't know faith in the positive, biblical sense, and has no experience of worship. This last (*prokynesis*) is certainly addressed to God, but also to the king, to the sovereign, the earthly lord, and above all to the heavenly and demonic powers. The perception is lacking that 'God alone is God'. But this, as I have said, is not mere ignorance. It has the self-same root as the sin of Lucifer, the prototype of those who, although knowing God, have neither given him glory nor given him thanks. This root consists in not wishing to exist by favour of anyone else, of not wishing to acknowledge oneself to be radically dependent, a creature. 'As long as I feel dependent, I am nothing.'[89] And that is what has been defined with philosophic rigour as 'desperately not wishing to be oneself', that is, a dependent creature.[90] 'Desperately', since any such effort has no possibility of succeeding (the Power that has brought us into existence being stronger than we are) and can only lead to despair.

The Apostle doesn't mean to say that all pagans without exception have lived in this type of sin. Further on, he speaks of pagans who follow the law of God engraved on their hearts (cf. Romans 2:14ff). He only means to say which sin is typical of pagans, that is to say, of people without biblical faith in God.

With the Fathers and with the liturgy of the Church, let us pray:

> O God to whom, whether we wish it or not, we all belong, and whom, whether we know it or not, we all love, by the strength of your love make our rebellious hearts obedient to your will.
>
> Through Christ our Lord.[91]

19   A tamed God

Having explained what the great irreligiousness and wickedness of the pagans consisted in, that is to say, in not acknowledging God as God and in not giving him glory and thanks, St Paul goes on to say that

> their arguments became futile and their uncomprehending minds were darkened. While they claimed to be wise, they were in fact growing so stupid that they exchanged the glory of the immortal God for an imitation, for the image of a mortal human being, or of birds, or animals, or reptiles (Romans 1:22–23).

Here we have an – at least implicit – reference to the creation story (cf. Genesis 1:26–27). There it says that God created human beings in his own image and likeness; here the Apostle says that, for God, the pagans have substituted the image and figure of a mortal human being. Idolatry, in other words, attempts to subvert what happened at the creation, a kind of reversal of roles: God makes humanity in his image; now humanity makes God in its image.

We are at the second phase or second stage of alienation from God now: idolatry. The Apostle sees this as the historical materialization and, so to speak, institutionalization of inner detachment from the Creator. What precisely happens in idolatry? Briefly, it is defined as 'worshipping the creature in place of the Creator'. At first sight, this might seem a simple error of perspective, or a substitution beyond question turning out to the total disadvantage of the worshipper, it being undoubtedly more rewarding to serve the master than the servant. But idolatry wouldn't be the frightful thing it is in the Bible, if it boiled down just to this. The decisive fact is that in worshipping the creature, human beings are adoring 'their' creature, the work of 'their hands', that is to say, themselves! In the ultimate analysis, they are putting themselves in place of God. At the root of all idolatry is autolatry, 'love of self carried to the point of scorn for God'.

It is an attempt to 'stifle the truth'. We do not just accept God, we make a God for ourselves; *we* do the deciding. The creatural relationship is turned upside down; we become the potter and God the pot which we mould as we please, attributing to God the ends and qualities that suit us best.

I should now like to show how this is very much the religious situation in which we find ourselves in the Western world, and one in which modern atheism has struck root. I have already laid out its basic theses, without however offering any reply to them. The moment has now come to do so. But 'with courtesy and respect', as Scripture exhorts us; in the spirit of one who seeks to give 'the reason for his own hope' (1 Peter 3:15), not as one who is squaring up to refute someone.

The instant answer to give people who say God doesn't exist but is a mere projection of the human mind, is they are right! Yes, God is truly, as they say, a product of the human mind. The problem however is to know which God we are talking about. What I hope to show is that these philosophers haven't fought and demolished the true God, but only an idol of God, an empty simulacrum.

At a given moment in the spiritual history of the West, the 'God of Sinai' has been replaced by a double of his, or his twin. As when a usurper gags and imprisons the true king in a secret tower, and then passes himself off as the king. When eventually the people stage a revolution and get rid of him too, they naively imagine they have liberated themselves from all kings and proclaim a republic. Saving the metaphor, they have proclaimed that God is dead.

Let's imagine that one day some loony were to smash up the statue of David by Michelangelo which stands in the square outside the Palazzo della Signoria in Florence, and were then to start shouting triumphantly: 'I've destroyed Michelangelo's David! David's done for! David's finished!' Poor deluded wretch, he doesn't know it was only a cast, a copy for hurrying tourists; the real Michelangelo David was taken out of the traffic ages ago and kept elsewhere, in a quieter place. Isn't this rather what happened with Nietzsche when, through one of his characters, he announced: 'We have killed God; we are his murderers!'?[92]

Now however we need to explain how and when this famous substitution took place, of which I speak. To understand, we need to go back to the episode of the golden calf, related in the Book of Exodus. The great sin of the golden calf, filling the Bible with outrage from one cover to the other – what exactly was it? It certainly wasn't avarice, in making gold one's God, as some people have thought; on the contrary, the Jews of old on occasion showed themselves amazingly generous with their gold. Nor did it consist in forsaking the Lord for some foreign deity, since the golden calf was acclaimed as the God of Israel, he who had brought the Chosen People out of Egypt, and the festival they organized was a festival 'in honour of the Lord' (cf. Exodus 32:4–5). Why then does Paul, and the whole Bible, call this act idolatry (cf. 1 Corinthians 10:7)? It is idolatry because the relationship between the Chosen People and their God has been changed. The people have made a golden calf for themselves so as to have 'a God who will walk at their head' (Exodus 32:1). That is to say, a kind of *labarum* or standard to carry in front of them and so come off best in engagements with their enemies. We know this was what the armies of antiquity did, and this, in later times, would be done with the Ark of the Covenant (cf. 1 Samuel 4:3ff). A God, in a word, to bring good luck, the *palladium* of the city. God had delivered the people from Egypt 'so that they could serve him in the wilds'; but now, rather than serving God, the people are making use of him. We are on the straight course towards superstition and magic: seizing God's power to use it for one's own advantage, not by means of prayer, but virtually out of arrogance.

The profound change that has taken place in the people's heart appears more clearly if we compare what happens round the God thus represented with what had happened in the presence of the Living God on Sinai. There the people had stood at a distance, full of sacred awe; here the people eat, drink, dance and actually organize a popular festival. They no longer stand in awe of him. God has been tamed. To grasp the difference between the Living God and the golden calf it is also helpful to read what happens a little later, once the simulacrum of God has been destroyed. In the next two chapters of Exodus, it is as though we are breathing the air of the divine and supernatural. As if God were once more free to act and make his awesome and joy-inspiring presence felt. God goes by, proclaims his name: 'The Lord, the Lord, God of tenderness and compassion ...' The human witness has to take cover in a hole, so as not to be destroyed, and be content with seeing God fleetingly and from behind. Moses bows to the ground. This is how God walks 'in the midst of his people' (cf. Exodus 34:9), not as a dead simulacrum.

Moses realized what mortal danger for true religion lay hidden in the incident of the golden calf. This is why he reacted so violently. He reduced the image to powder, threw the powder into the water and made the Israelites swallow it. Undoubtedly the great biblical prohibition against making images and physical representations of God came into existence or was reinforced owing to this episode.

Now let us pray in the words of Paul Claudel:

> Blessed be you, my God, who have set me free from idols
> and will have it that I worship you alone,
> and not Isis and Osiris instead,
> or Justice, or Progress, or Truth,
> or Divinity, or Humanity,
> or the Laws of Nature, or Art, or Beauty,
> or the Void left by your absence.[93]

20 The God of Abraham and the God of the philosophers

The attempt at 'taming' God didn't, alas! come to an end that day on the slopes of Mount Sinai. It has accompanied the human race throughout its history, taking various forms, one of which is precisely what has led to the present crisis which we are examining. With the advance and refining of the religious sensibility, the mode in which or the material of which the idol is made has changed, but not the substance of the thing. No longer an exterior, visible idol, but an interior, invisible one; no longer an idol of gold, silver or marble, but a spiritual idol, the idea of God! We make our own idea of God (a thing thus far lawful and even necessary), we work it over and without noticing, by degrees, we end by substituting (a thing, this last, neither lawful nor necessary) our idea for the reality.

If we want to grasp what, in this case, happens between the human soul and God, let us imagine this scenario. A king consents to pose for his portrait. Little by little, as the king's image takes shape on the canvas, the painter gets ever more taken with it, walks round and round it, gazing at it in rapture. Until,

when the work is finished, he is so enthusiastic, he ends by forget-
ting all about the king sitting there and turns his back on him, so
anxious is he to show his friends the qualities of the portrait he
has painted. But the matter doesn't end here. The artist's disciples
start making copies of the portrait, each modifying and adapting
it according to personal style and taste. Others draw copies of
these copies. By now the portrait is on every street corner, but by
now so far removed from the real thing that when the king goes
by incognito, nobody recognizes him any more.

The word 'idol' (*eidolon*) is revealing. It has come to mean,
in common parlance, a material object venerated as God, or, in a
figurative sense, things and values (such as sex, money, fame and
so forth) to which people attach an exaggerated importance, so
that they become the be-all and end-all of their lives. But, properly speaking, 'idol' has the same etymology as 'idea' and, in
practice, the two things are often confused. In learned acceptance, the *eidola* are the images interposed between the thinking
subject and reality; they are the mental pictures, which can be the
means by which we know the reality, but which can easily
become veils between us and that reality, surrogates, if they are
detached from the reality in question. 'Prejudices' Francis Bacon
called them in his famous list of *idola, tribus, specus, fori, theatri*,
that is to say, prejudices inherent to human nature in general, to
the individual, to language, and to schools or systems.

The idea, the concept, as fruit of the intelligence, is certainly
the noblest thing that can be in human nature, before grace, but
as always the best of things if corrupted becomes the worst,
corruptio optimi pessima, as they used to say in Latin.

So there is a form of religious idolatry which doesn't consist
in making a God for oneself out of exterior pictures or images
like the golden calf, but in making interior, mental, invisible
images of him and substituting this image (which is one's idea of
God) for the real Living God and being satisfied with this. In this

form, idolatry has not been diminishing over the centuries, but on the contrary has been growing, to reach a climax where faith in God has been replaced by the ideology of God, that is to say, a philosophy detached from the real thing and developed abstractly on its own given premises. Ideo-logy is the modern form of ideo-latry.

What is the difference between God and the idea of God? The difference is that, on its own, the idea doesn't exist. God exists! An infinite difference. In the prophets, the divine name 'I am here', which was revealed to Moses in the burning bush, is often used to mark the difference between Yahweh and the idols (cf. Isaiah 42:8; 45:18). It is as though God wished to say: I truly exist and bring into existence; I am not an inert, insubstantial God like the idols of the nations.

Another difference between God and the idea of God is that there is only one Living God, but as many ideas of God as there are people to think or speculate about him. The person is one, alone, but the photographs or portraits of him run to infinity. God is the whole, whereas the idea only ever represents one little part.

The Living God is a God who 'scrutinizes' you while you are scrutinizing him; he knows all your thoughts even before they are formed (cf. Psalm 139:1ff). The idea of God can't do any of this. The Living God can't be controlled, comprehended; the idea of God, even the idea of the Living God, can.

This distinction between the reality and the idea of God in certain respects recalls the distinction between the Living God and the 'God of the philosophers'. Both the Living God and the God of the philosophers are called the God of someone. The Living God is called 'the God of Abraham, of Isaac and Jacob'; the God of the philosophers is called the God of Descartes, Kant and Hegel ... But it's a matter of two completely different ways of speaking. In the former case, God is the subject, in the latter he is the object; the first is a subjective genitive, the second is an objective genitive. In the first case we are talking about the God who revealed himself to Abraham and had chosen him: here God is the protagonist, not Abraham. In the second, we are talking of the God whom Descartes, Kant and Hegel had thought up, about whom they philosophized. Here the philosopher and not God is the protagonist. Some difference!

'The God of the philosophers and the learned', writes Blondel,

> is the entity of reason, reached and hypothesized by an intellectual method, considered as explanatory or existential principle, which they have the gall to define or even to influence, like some object one might possess in the representation one makes of it. The God of Abraham is that mysterious and good being who freely reveals something of his unfathomable perfections, who is not reached by the intellect alone, in whom we recognize an intimate reality, inaccessible to our natural grasp, and before whom the beginning of wisdom can only be awe and humility. At the same time, however, he is the God who, by revealing the secrets of his life to the human race, sets it apart from his own divinity, calls it to exchange the natural, servile condition of creature for friendship, for supernatural adoption as his child, orders it to love him and only give itself to him who gives himself to it.[94]

Yet, even though distinct, the God of Abraham and the God of the philosophers are not *per se* entirely incompatible. The actual expression 'God of the philosophers' didn't come into being in opposition to the God of the Bible; on the contrary, it was intended to mean this God, even though in a polemical context. To the Marcionite gnostics who took offence at the 'passions' of the God of the Old Testament, Tertullian retorts:

> Whatever attributes you require of God must be found in the
> Father, who is invisible, unapproachable, placid, and (so to
> speak) the God of the philosophers (*philosophorum deus*);
> whereas those qualities which you censure as unworthy must
> be supposed to be in the incarnate or about-to-be incarnate
> Son.[95]

At a much deeper and more constructive level, reconciliation
between the Living God and the God of the philosophers was
undertaken and brought to a good end by St Thomas Aquinas.
Defining God as 'the Self-subsistent Being', he bridged the gap
between the God of Aristotle, 'the first cause, unmoved yet
moving all things', and the God of the Bible and Christian tradition, conceived precisely (in the light of deeper and deeper understanding of Exodus 3:14) as 'He who is'.

Pascal too, in his *Memorial* quoted above, took up
Tertullian's expression and made it famous, intending to distinguish between the two but not to set them in opposition to each
other. His phrase: 'God of Abraham . . . not of the philosophers
and the learned' is only a paraphrase of Christ's own words: 'I
bless you, Father, Lord of heaven and earth, for hiding these
things from the learned and the clever . . .' (Matthew 11:25). He
was not therefore an irrationalist who rejected the function of the
reason in the search for God; only, in this case, he subordinates
philosophy to revelation. There haven't been many periods in all
these centuries when believers have wanted to do without the
God of the philosophers; mostly it's been the philosophers
who've wanted to get rid of the God of the believers.

Let us pray in the words of a famous hymn by St Gregory
Nazianzen, that these will help us recover a true sense of the
Living God, a sense that is above reason but not contrary to it:

O you who are beyond all!
How else can we call you?
How can words speak of you who are the Ineffable?
Or the mind contemplate you who are the Incomprehensible?
You the Nameless One from whom all names derive,
You the Unknown One from whom all knowledge comes!

You are killing a dead God!

We have now reached the acme of the process of reducing the Living God to our own idea of God – hence the crisis which we have described above: let us see how this has come about. In a sense, the process is natural enough and always going on, but it has accelerated in modern times, starting with Descartes.

With this philosopher, things get turned upside down: knowing gets the upper hand over being; gnoseology – to use the technical term – wins out over ontology. The baseline or foundation of all is not: 'God is', but 'I am'. At the base of all is no longer the great 'I Am' of God, but the little 'I am' of the individual. 'I think, therefore I am', not: 'God thinks (and loves too) and therefore I am'. The baseline has been displaced and with it the centre of gravity of everything: from reality to thought, from object to subject. 'The existence of God,' says Descartes, 'is demonstrated *a posteriori* by the fact that the idea of him exists in us.' Here the idea of God leaps into the foreground and seats itself on the very throne of God.

In this view of things, God is reduced to the 'innate idea'

that we have of him, which may be defined as the mother-idea of all others but is still only an idea. God doesn't present and doesn't impose himself primarily as reality, but as the idea of a reality, albeit the most sublime of realities. He doesn't appear as he without whom we couldn't exist, but as he without whom we couldn't think, the idea of God being that which underpins all the others. St Paul says that 'in him we live and move and exist' (cf. Acts 17:28); but here we say that God is he in whom, and thanks to whom, we think. He is, primarily, the foundation of our rational thought and, only secondarily, of our existence. The reversal may seem a fine one; make no doubt about it however, its effects are incalculable.

We would not wish to pass judgment on the value or perti-nence of this process in itself (we can leave this to our friends the philosophers); nor would we want to deny its founder the merit of having introduced a more rigorous method of philosophic reasoning. What we do wish to show however are the negative repercussions this has had on the development of the faith and the religious spirit.

As is so often the case, the effects weren't to emerge immedi-ately, for Descartes was himself a religious man. He was a reli-gious thinker and wanted to put the faith on a firm basis, not demolish it. But the process had begun. It would only later need someone – it was to be Kant – to take the next step, by stating that from a God 'who is thought' there is no passing on to a God who exists, that from the idea of God we can never deduce his 'reality',[96] and it will soon be seen with what consequences such a change of perspective was fraught.

With this step, we arrive at the absolute idealism of Hegel, where 'the Idea is a Creator God who, in creating, creates himself'. The idea of God at this point has become independent of the reality; it isn't caused by the reality, but causes it, gives rise to it. The roles are inverted. The Living God is left outside this system of thought; the system of thought has itself taken his place. The *eidolon* of God has become the substitute for God. The idea has been 'absolutized', that is to say, proclaimed as the Absolute. Thus we find the situation of *autolatria* reproduced which the Apostle diagnosed as lying beneath pagan *idolatria*. Our contemporaries, Péguy observes, adore themselves under the species of a God who is turn by turn 'intellectual, historical or sociological'.

What has happened to the Living God is like what happens to the old king in the tragedy: first he is welcomed with royal honours at the castle (here the human mind) and then, once inside, the gates having been closed and the drawbridges raised, unarmed and deprived of his escort, he is murdered in his sleep. Macbeth takes his king's place. The substitution we spoke of earlier is thus completed: the true God's place has been taken by his double.

At this point occurs what we mentioned earlier. Feuerbach arrives and explodes the whole process by attacking the very 'idea of God' at its root. God doesn't exist, the reality of the idea of God (in so far as there is anything real about it) isn't a distinct, superior, infinite Being, but humanity itself. Human beings, in a word, have created God in their own image. Thus he brings to a conclusion the programme laid out by his master Hegel in one of his youthful writings:

> After all the efforts of the past, one conquest has been reserved for our own days: to reclaim, at least in principle, as the property of the human race, the treasures transferred to heaven. But which generation will have the courage to enforce this right by reappropriating what belongs to it?[97]

Feuerbach is the one who had this 'courage'. He 'proclaimed from the housetops' what the master (perhaps held back by the rigid measures still being taken in his day against anyone at odds with official orthodoxy) had confined himself to 'whispering in the ear' of the restricted few admitted to his more secret teachings.

No one is better placed than a Christian believer to appreciate the very profound truth and relevance there is in the foregoing operation, and we may indeed feel grateful to the man who carried it to a conclusion. Merely because it doesn't strike at the faith, but at idolatry. The process of formation of belief in God which he unmasks is precisely that process underlying idolatry, as the Apostle had implicitly stated. In idolatry, human beings make a God in their own image.

Conditioned as he was by the debate in progress between the philosophic schools of his own day, Feuerbach, without being aware of it, mistook the image for the reality: the deformed and emptied image of the Christian faith, for the Christian faith. He had not, as he believed, exposed 'the essence of Christianity', but the essence of idolatry, or of the ideology of God.

That Feuerbach's criticism applies to idolatry and not to true faith in the Living God is something that is now recognized even by thinkers by no means suspect of being apologists for Christianity. 'Man', writes Erik Fromm,

> transfers his own passions and qualities to the idol. The more he empties himself, the bigger and stronger the idol becomes. The idol is the alienated form of man's experience of himself. By worshipping it, man worships himself . . . He depends on the idol because only by subjecting himself to it can he find the shadow, even though not the substance, of himself. The idol is a thing and has no life. God, on the contrary, is a Living God.[98]

The most certain proof that the theorists of modern atheism haven't been able to hit the Living God, their target, is that they do not know who he is. They know the God of the schools, of the systems, of such-and-such a master, but the God of the faith lived by true believers, hardly at all. They know the God of books, but the Living God is not so much encountered in books as in the lives of people – for a living being cannot be contained in dead things.

A clear sign we are no longer in the presence of the Living God of revelation is the disappearance of any reference to the Trinity. The trinitarian dogma is declared 'in practical terms irrelevant for human beings' (Kant), or for the Trinity conceived in biblical terms as *fellowship*, is substituted a trinity conceived, philosophically, as *becoming* and as *dialectic* (Hegel), which is almost its complete opposite. (There cannot be loving fellowship between a trinity of persons who, succeeding one another in 'an eternal becoming' can at most love one another 'in anticipation', but not in reality.)

It would not have been so easy to reduce God to a mirage produced by contemplating one's own essence, if the starting point had been God, the ineffable fellowship of trinitarian love. What need would human beings then have had to divide and 'triplicate' themselves into Father, Son and Holy Spirit?

But in this, the responsibility of Christians too immediately leaps to the eye. For they it was who abetted this sad conclusion, in as much as, little by little, they lost a sense of the living, pulsating reality of the Trinity, in favour of the vague concept of 'deity' or 'divine essence' which smoothed the way to 'deism'; or in as much as they allowed God from *Being* to decline little by little into *Entity*, the famous 'Supreme Entity' of so many vague discourses about God, in which God himself turned into a '*Deus vagus*', a vague, generic God.

The fathers of atheism therefore didn't know the God of the great tradition of the Church, but only the aseptic God in circulation in university circles. They knew practically nothing of the holy and 'mysterious' God, the one who proclaims in the Bible: 'My thoughts are not your thoughts and your ways are not my ways' (Isaiah 55:8), the God who wrenches from the lips of someone who *has* known him the agonizing words: 'You make my flesh tremble with fear', or again: 'My God, my God, why have you forsaken me?' (Psalm 22:1). The God to whom a Jewish believer could, before dying, address this terrible cry, found written on the wall inside a house burnt out in one of all too many of history's pogroms: 'O God, you have done everything to make me lose my faith. But you haven't succeeded!' Or, if they did know this God, thanks to their knowledge of the Bible, they were unable to integrate him into their philosophical system.

A God like this: they too should have realized that no human being could possibly have invented him, being entirely other from what human beings might have thought God to be, if left to themselves. He isn't 'useful'. Far from backing up our desires and fancies, he upsets us and completely 'darkens' our mind, even though for the purpose of making us happier.

The difference between God and this his surrogate is boundless. The God of the Bible doesn't start whining at human beings who mean to abandon him (as Sartre's God does in the play *Les Mouches*); he doesn't go begging for followers and recognition like founders we might name of new and counterfeit religions. He doesn't wheedle: 'Please, please, believe in me!' but rather with calm and sovereign authority says: 'Be still and *know* that I am God,' as we noted at the beginning of our book. 'Whether you like it or not, whether you believe it or not, I am God.'

'We are taught God by the prophets and by Christ,' says Tertullian, 'not by the philosophers, nor by Epicurus.'[99] When a philosopher, wanting to know who God is, confines himself to questioning other philosophers, he is like a map-maker consulting another map-maker about the features of a region which neither of them has ever visited, where neither of them has ever set foot. Inevitably they substitute the map for the terrain, as the saying goes.

'You are killing a dead man,' said a famous, wounded *condottiere* to the enemy about to finish him off. To anyone proclaiming today that God is dead and boasting he himself has killed him, or to anyone who adds that God has died 'without even having to stand trial',[100] a believer could quite justifiably reply, 'You are killing a dead God!'

That this sort of God is dead pleases us too, and we must make very sure we don't try to bring him back to life. The idol is the very negation of the Living God. In as much however as these philosophers have not really been fighting against the Living God, but only his semblance, their atheism isn't a negation of God, but a negation of the negation of God. They have in some degree smoothed the way to rediscovery of the Living God. They are our allies, rather than our enemies.

Bonhoeffer's critique of the so-called Stopgap-God goes basically in the same direction and is exquisitely biblical and 'Mosaic', in that the Stopgap-God of the Christians is very close – in the purposes he serves – to what the golden calf was for the Jews in the desert. Provided always that from such a critique we do not draw the ambiguous conclusion that we ought to get used to living *etsi Deus non daretur*, as though God didn't exist. For this neither Moses nor the Bible ever dreamed of saying.

Let us do our best to dilate our minds to the limitless dimensions of the true God by making ours these lines from St Gregory Nazianzen's hymn to the Almighty:

> All that can babble and all that cannot, praise you,
> All that can think and all that cannot, worship you.
> The world's yearning and groaning is directed to you,
> To you rises the universal prayer;
> Contemplating your works,
> Every being raises a silent hymn to you.

22   Truth and research

Where, in what we have been talking about so far, is that element which St Paul in Romans 1:18 calls 'ungodliness' and 'injustice'? It lies in the fact that, once again, the moderns have, to a given degree, completely lost the feeling that one cannot speak about God without also bowing the knees of the heart, without also giving him glory and thanks, consenting that he should remain the Living God. Nowadays people don't speak of him for *his* glory, but for *theirs*.

The roles have been reversed. God has had to serve to assure the success of the philosopher and, we shall see, sometimes even the theologian. Hence the climate of dispute between personalities and schools, in which God himself was pushed into second place. God was no more a *person*, but an *argument*. Doxology lost its force, humble thanksgiving, worship, things which when they are in the writer's heart manifest themselves even when not expressed. This evil then is the same as that of pagan philosophy: lack of humility. You often hear talk of the 'uneasiness' in our civilization. By the light of the Word of God, we see this uneasiness has a precise cause: pride.

It's not hard to single out some of the main reasons leading in modern times to this loss of a sense of the infinite qualitative difference between God and human kind; hence, to the loss of doxology and worship even among Christians. The first is a certain one-sided insistence on the fact of the incarnation and immanence of God, as though with this God ceased to be God, whereas we know that at the incarnation 'God became what he was not, while remaining what he was.'

But more than the incarnation and the self-humbling of God what has produced all this is an undue self-exaltation of the human, i.e. humanism, understood as the system that puts the human being at the centre of the universe and apex of all. God, says Tertullian, by taking flesh, 'subtracted something from himself to confer it on man'.[101] And we have done the opposite; we have taken something away from God to confer it on ourselves.

To this fact be added the elevation of the search for truth to pride of place, higher even than truth itself. 'If God', wrote Lessing, that proponent of the Enlightenment,

> were to grasp all truth in his right hand, and in his left, only the ever-living aspiration to the truth, were it even on condition of my being eternally wrong, and he were to say to me: 'Choose!', I should humbly bow down towards the left saying 'This one, Father! Pure truth belongs to you alone'.[102]

The pleasure of the chase is far superior to the pleasure of possessing the prey, Lessing himself adduced in justification, as though what counted in this field were pleasure and not, contrariwise, duty.

Beneath a show of humility, and with the excuse of not ever wanting to be 'sure of self', this position masks the greatest human pride. As long as one is in search of the truth, the researcher is the protagonist, not the truth. The 'veracity', that is to say, the sincerity of the search, honesty with oneself, becomes more important than the truth. Scripture told us long ago of those who are 'always seeking learning, but unable ever to come to knowledge of the truth' (cf. 2 Timothy 3:7). It is a neat attempt to hold God in check. For, like this, one can spend a whole lifetime in doing research about God, without ever worshipping him. It's like someone spending years and years doing accounts over and over again, so as to put off repayment of a debt. I remember these infinitely sad words confided to me at the deathbed of someone who had spent his life writing and lecturing about God: 'I have spent my life doing research on God but have never searched for God!'

As long as research is the order of the day, the researcher, as I said, calls the tune. But when the Truth with a capital letter has been found, then Truth it is that leaps upon the throne and lays down the law; and the researcher must be the first to fall on his or her knees. And this is the moment many learned folk seek to put off as long as they can, indefinitely. What Dostoevsky says in general terms applies too to research about God:

> Man only loves the process by which he reaches the end, and not the end itself . . . He crosses oceans, sacrifices a lifetime in this research, but to discover, actually to find, he is as though afraid.[103]

I believe the success now being enjoyed by so many extra-biblical cults is to be explained, at least in part, by what we are now saying. The feature shared by almost all these new religions is to preach an impersonal God, Absolute Spirit, vital force, cosmic law, the All or, as it may be, the Nothing, and so on. The main difference between the personal and an impersonal God is that the former has a will we have to reckon with, to which we must submit; the latter has not. To bow before an impersonal God costs nothing; you might as well bow down to yourself. You will not hear those *Thou shalts* and those *Thou shalt nots*, which people find so upsetting, but neither will you hear the words: 'I have loved you with an everlasting love' and 'Enter into the joy of your Lord.'

'The Absolute', a philosopher has said, 'kills research.' 'The Absolute', says another, 'kills the conscience.' 'Omnipotence', adds a third, 'annuls freedom.' But the Absolute kills human pride, not the human being, nor his or her research. For even once Truth has been found, research goes on, yes, then more passionately than ever (for a vast field has opened up in which to 'search'), but it is now carried on by believers.

Divine omnipotence doesn't annul freedom; on the contrary, it creates and makes it possible. 'The highest thing that can be done for a being,' says Kierkegaard,

> much higher than what a man could do, is to make him free. To be able to do this, omnipotence is precisely what is needed. This seems strange since omnipotence, you might think, would make people dependent . . . One man can never make another man completely free . . . Only omnipotence can restrain itself while giving, and this relationship exactly constitutes the independence of the recipient. All finite power makes people dependent; only omnipotence can make them independent.[104]

In other words, only with God are we truly free.

Let us pray with the last two verses of St Gregory Nazianzen's hymn to the Almighty:

Thanks to you the universe subsists,
towards you all things hasten;
of everything you are the goal,
you the One, you the All, yet no one;
being neither one nor all things,
by what name shall I call you,
Nameless One, bearer of every name?

What angelic intelligence could pierce
through the darkness beyond the clouds?
Oh, be merciful, you who are beyond all!
What otherwise can I call you?[105]

23   Faith doesn't have propositions as its term

It wouldn't be very honest of us if we were to confine ourselves to denouncing the form of idolatry that has developed in secular culture and philosophy and not draw attention to other forms of it which have wormed their way into the Church itself among us believers. St Thomas Aquinas laid down the great principle: 'Faith doesn't have a proposition as its term, but a reality.' When the formulae of faith – including those most solemn ones, the dogmas – start being handed down and accepted for their own sakes, without their opening every time, like doors, to give access to the living reality of God and Jesus Christ, when they, so to speak, become fossilized, we arrive at formalism, which is the equivalent of ideology among practising Christians. The formulae about God then become what is often the idea of God held by the philosophers: the surrogate of the Living God, faded and neutralized copies of the reality. The names and definitions are a bit like the lines of latitude and longitude on the world map. They help us take our bearings (and in this respect are valuable and necessary), but what folly if they were ultimately to reduce the earth to that grid, so that we couldn't for a moment in future imagine it without them!

The evolution taking place in our view of the task of theology has certainly had an influence on all this. We now have excellent studies reconstructing the evolution of the meaning of the word 'theology' from earliest times to our own day. These studies have revealed a very clear development and a sort of rupture occurring round about the twelfth century. Up to this date, theology means 'a certain way of knowing God and of speaking about him'. A way marked by praise, worship, full acceptance of God into one's own life. At times the term *theologia*, which means speaking about God, seems virtually synonymous with *theosebeia*, which means worshipping God.[106]

In one of the earliest Christian texts in which the verb 'theologize' (*theologein*) occurs, it means 'to proclaim Christ as God by means of hymns and canticles'.[107] For Origen, theologians are first of all the Prophets, then John the Baptist (since he proclaimed the divinity of Christ) and above all Christ himself when he speaks of the Father. St John the Evangelist was known to tradition as 'the Theologian', once again because in elevated manner he proclaimed the divinity of the Word. Theology is seen mainly as a wisdom, a grace, a charism. Only the Holy Spirit, who delves into the depths of God, can teach one how to speak about God. Evagrius in the fourth century formulated the famous equation: 'If you are a theologian, you will pray truly, and if you pray truly, you will be a theologian.'[108]

Beginning from the twelfth century with the introduction of Abelard's dialectic and Aristotelian philosophy into the sacred science, theology acquires a new significance: that of an organized and learned knowledge of the data of revelation, a reasoned exposition of what concerns the Christian faith, as St Thomas defines it in the prologue to his *Summa*. In this sense we may speak of a 'Sum of Theology', that is, an organized, coherent totality of the questions with bearing on God and revelation. In a word, the concept of theology as science is born.[109]

At the time when this change took place, there was nothing particularly revolutionary about it. For it didn't exclude that religious component of humble submission to God which had been linked time out of mind with theological activity. But the innate danger in this new way of conceiving of theology didn't take long in making itself felt, in the period following that of the great masters of Scholasticism, with the triumph of so-called Nominalism. In this movement, dominating the field in the fourteenth and fifteenth centuries,

> theology becomes an opportunity for demonstrating one's ability in the practice of the art of logic. It lacks, that is to say, an inner relationship with the object. Theology ceases to be the doctrine of salvation, and the theologian can all the more easily abandon himself to bold speculation, the less he sees his personal salvation to be involved in his theological system.[110]

So here one can no longer speak of genuine theology, but at most of theological virtuosity. True, almost all the theses peculiar to this school were subsequently to be abandoned, but the lost ground has never been quite recovered, nor has the method of theologizing then introduced ever been entirely abandoned.

In Nominalism, ideas began losing contact with substance, becoming reduced in effect to mere 'names', which could be manipulated at will, being by now devoid of any real content and no longer anchored in 'things', that is to say, in salvation-history. It was the clearest possible contradiction of the principle that 'Faith doesn't have propositions as its term, but things.'

Another fact should also be borne in mind as accounting for the negative evolution of theology conceived as 'science'. In the days of St Thomas and St Bonaventure, theology was the queen of the sciences and was accorded pride of place over all other disciplines in the universities. Theology it was that 'informed' the other sciences, while in any case, they too, were still conceived of in a sacral and religious key. The difficulty was to become apparent later when, rightly, the sciences broke free – and relationships changed as a result. The science *par excellence* becomes philosophy and, eventually, in recent centuries, physics. At this point, it is the other sciences which imperceptibly impose their own scientific code on theology, especially when the latter is professed side by side with all the other disciplines in lay universities. For one of the postulates of scientific procedure is that the scientist be impartial in relation to the object of his research; furthermore that he master it, have command of it. When a scientist is to be eulogized, he is said to have perfect 'mastery' of his material. To have command of the object that is known is part, as we have seen, of knowledge itself, as it is conceived of in the Western world, in the Greek philosophical tradition.

But when this scientific principle, which is more than valid elsewhere, is applied to theology, it suddenly seems misplaced. How can one 'master' God or Holy Writ? In this unique case, the object is above the subject, that is to say, the enquirer, and cannot be mastered, nor can one remain neutral before it. But this is what has happened on a grand scale, in such a slow and pervasive way that the problem is rarely noticed. Especially in dealing with Scripture and the word of God, teachers have frequently succumbed to this danger.

Generally speaking, theology has lost its spiritual component, which in time past permeated it completely. To some degree a need has been felt to recover this dimension, and to do this an independent discipline has been instituted called 'spiritual theology', but which remains optional nonetheless. It too has quickly taken on a scientific format, hence objective and neutral.

The very concept of 'edifying' gets tendentiously disqualified as something belonging to an inferior category – so-called edifying literature – to be left for pious creeps! Whereas it has been said, and I believe, quite rightly that 'from the Christian point of view, everything, absolutely everything, should serve for edification. The sort of learning which is not in the last resort edifying is precisely for that reason unchristian'.[1] The idea of letting out an exclamation of astonishment and praise in the midst of discoursing about God, as St Paul often does, today would seem somewhat absurd, unscientific, hardly serious-minded. Yet it would be in the perfect logic of things.

The theologian should never be like the geographer in Saint-Exupéry's *Little Prince*.

> 'Your planet is very beautiful,' says the little prince. 'Has it any oceans?'
>
> 'I couldn't tell you,' the geographer replies.
>
> 'Are there towns, and rivers, and deserts?'
>
> 'I couldn't tell you that either,' says the geographer.
>
> 'But you are a geographer!'
>
> 'Exactly,' says the geographer, 'but I am not an explorer. It's not the geographer's job to go out and count the towns, the rivers, the mountains, the seas, the oceans and the deserts. The geographer is too important a person to go loafing about. He does not leave his desk. But he receives the explorers in his study. He asks them questions and he notes down what they recall of their travels.'

The theologian can't excuse himself from praying; for the rivers, mountains, seas, oceans and deserts of the 'planet' God, can't be explored except in prayer.

If the sin denounced by St Paul consists in knowing God but in not at the same time giving him the glory and thanks that are his due, then we can't avoid the conclusion that the Apostle's saying also passes judgment – and perhaps above all – on a certain way of doing theology which has been going on for centuries in Europe as the main way, and been exported by us to the rest of the world.

There has been change since the Second Vatican Council, there was even before it. Theology has sought to come nearer to the human being and God's people's concrete problems, in a word, to return to 'things'. Its input is impressive in many fields and its function health-giving and indispensable for the life of the Church. What would become of Christian spirituality without a sound and rational theology to protect it from the snares of subjectivism and non-commitment? But much remains to be done in the other direction, that by which theology first of all draws nearer – and nearer – to God. 'Nothing', says an ancient author, 'is more impoverished than the thought which enquires into the things of God, outside God.'[112]

To bring this meditation to a close, let us too say the prayer St Thomas Aquinas used to recite before setting about his theological studies:

> Grant, we beseech you, O merciful God,
> that we may ardently desire what is pleasing to you,
> may investigate it prudently,
> discover it unerringly
> and fervently put it into practice
> to the praise and glory of your name. Amen.[113]

24 Which of us can dwell among perpetual flames?

What we have said about theological formulae should also be said about other ecclesial realities, such as ceremonies and the hierarchy. A danger analogous to that incurred with 'representations' of God is incurred with God's 'representatives' too. God's representatives are individuals, structures, authorities, mediations, acting on God's behalf, and in the Church there are plenty of them. These too, if imperceptibly they become detached from the unique reality and authority they represent, if they lose their humble, instrumental character, if they take for granted that they always in whatever circumstances represent the will and thought of God, they too end up assuming a more or less accentuated aspect of idolatry. The idolizing of authority, of structures, even (at least in the past) of the Magisterium.

Who would be bold enough to say we're talking of a purely hypothetical danger? When one claims to shut God and his living will inside a closed system of dogmas, laws, institutions and canons, with everything cut and dried, inevitably the sense of the Living God gets lost.

The signs, starting with the sacramental ones, the mediations, the formulae, are necessary, nay, essential in Christianity precisely so that God and Jesus Christ do not get reduced to abstract ideas; but these too need to be purified, renewed in the Spirit, so as not to turn into 'flesh that serves for nothing' and 'the letter that kills'. St Thomas says that 'even the Gospel letter kills unless the healing grace of faith is present within'.[114] So what's to be said about other 'letters' a lot less sacred than the Gospel?

In this connection there is I think another sphere I ought to mention where vigilance is needed not to fall into idolatry: that of so-called popular religion. The golden calf was a typical case of popular religion. The Israelites came thronging round Aaron the priest, demanding: 'Make us a God to go at our head!' Aaron replied: 'Strip off the gold rings in the ears of your wives and daughters, and bring them to me.' How often this scene is repeated in various parts of Christendom, with the statue of the patron saint for instance! Obviously popular religion is good, worthy of respect, if it serves to express in ways dear to people's hearts authentic Christian faith in the Living God and Jesus Christ. But if the fiesta and the procession in honour of the patron saint, or of some event or other, is the high spot of the whole liturgical year, the most solemnly felt moment, even outdoing Easter, then something needs correcting there. It's no good saying what Aaron said to Moses in order to justify himself: 'The people wanted it' (cf. Exodus 32:22ff).

Despite these critical observations, I am not saying that everything in recent centuries has become ideology, formalism, outside and inside the Church, and hence idolatry in the sense explained above, as though the Living God had disappeared from the life of the Church as well as from secular culture and philosophy. I have only sought, following step by step the guidance and authority of St Paul, to point out a negative component, like a dark vein in a seam of pure gold, which has to be got rid of so that the gold can gleam in all its splendour. Sometimes we are only talking of a danger, or of a threat which must be guarded against. As iron and almost everything in contact with agents in the atmosphere will oxidize, so the faith in contact with our minds, our lives and culture, tends to get covered in human incrustations. From time to time this layer of oxidization has to be removed, so that it may recover its shine.

This is nothing to be surprised at, however. The tendency to make golden calves for ourselves and make protective spaces between ourselves and God is an aspect of our human condition, ever since Adam, having sinned for the first time, felt the need to 'hide' among the trees when God arrived (cf. Genesis 3:10). In the Book of Samuel, the people's proposal to send the Lord's ark away is justified by this telling sentence: 'Who can stand his ground before this holy God?' (1 Samuel 6:20). Isaiah reports what the godless and the sinners in Sion used to say or think: 'Which of us can dwell beside a devouring fire? Which of us can dwell among perpetual flames?' (Isaiah 33:14).

People who often have to go amid the flames, firemen for instance, wear (or at least used to wear) asbestos, fire-repellent suits. With God, we do the same. The 'asbestos suit' may be the idea, the formula, the ceremony, signs, human traditions, all sorts of things. Everything in a word that acts as an insulator between us and the devouring fire which is God. And the Church with its culture, organization, history, can become the shield behind which we take shelter to avoid the 'burning' confrontation with the Living God, rather than the place where this encounter should occur.

Isaiah responds, in that passage, by pointing out what one must do to survive amid the perpetual flames: 'One must act uprightly and speak honestly . . .' But this is precisely what people don't feel inclined to do. St John in his Gospel says the same thing, using the imagery of light: 'God is light' (1 John 1:5) 'but people have preferred darkness to the light because their deeds were evil' (John 3:19).

But there is a reason which perhaps comes even before all this. A great theologian following in the steps of St Thomas Aquinas explains our unwillingness to accept the divine as being due to our own proud wish to 'leave God to his divine concerns, so as not to be disturbed in our own human ones'.[115] And that this may not be just a theologian's abstract conjecture is, for instance, demonstrated by those terrible lines of Goethe's, significantly entitled: 'Human feeling':

> O you Gods, great Gods
> who dwell in spacious heaven
> grant us on earth firm minds and brave hearts!
> And we shall gladly leave you
> the spacious heavens above.[116]

In other words, human beings seek protection within their boundaries. We make our creatural limitations into a defence against the Infinite. We realize that in the presence of the Living God we cannot behave as bosses but only in humility as a virtually subject race, and we try to escape from this situation. We want to run our own show!

The diminishing of the sense of the Living God, its progressive replacement by the idea of God or by other surrogates, is not therefore due to God. It is not a kind of spiritual equivalent of the physical law of entropy, by which for instance radioactive bodies tend, with time, to lose the intensity of their radiation and become burnt out. Rather, it is a consequence of what the Apostle called ungodliness. In proportion as glorification of and thanksgiving to God diminishes, that is to say, practical and devout acknowledgment of God, God himself hides, is reduced to a dead simulacrum. As when a volcano becomes extinct and the stream of white-hot lava which used to flow from its crater turns to stone.

Let us pray with the author of *The Imitation of Christ*:

> The children of Israel of old said to Moses: 'Speak to us and we will listen, but do not let the Lord speak to us, for fear we should die' (Exodus 20:19). Not so, O Lord, not so, I pray, but rather: Let not Moses speak to me, nor any of the prophets, but rather speak to me yourself, Lord God, Inspirer and Enlightener of all the prophets.[117]

25 Recognize God's right to freedom!

In conclusion, we should make up our minds to leave God his freedom. The world demands human freedom; but only talks about it. Above all, human freedom *vis-à-vis* God, revelation, his law. We must cry out: Recognize God's right to freedom! just as one of the psalmists cries: 'Acknowledge the power of God!' (Psalm 68:34).

What does it mean to recognize or restore God's freedom? It means accepting him as the God ever new, who is always doing new things even before we have managed to understand the old ones (which, however, we shall never manage to grasp completely). It means not constricting him to our pace. This is the temptation for the Church in its human element: wanting to 'systematize' God, that is, to reduce him to a watertight system, ready to be handed down, with nothing pending, in good working order. The Church is like a publisher with a genius to deal with. The genius has begun a large-scale novel, having arranged with the publisher that the latter will bring it out in instalments. Little by little as the writer goes on, the work grows broader in scope, new characters emerge, new episodes, and earlier episodes are taken up again and improved . . . There seems no end to his artistic creativity. But the publisher gets more and more impatient. He would like the work completely finished, so that he can bind it up into a handsome volume, put it in his catalogue and distribute it. Instead he is obliged to keep reprinting, since readers all want the latest version and he, the poor publisher, doesn't get a chance to sell the old stock stacked in his warehouses.

I think we are stingy with God over his freedom; the tendency is so inborn in us that we aren't even aware of it. Where is the God who claims the right to plant and uproot, to build and pull down, to wound and heal, to send to hell and bring back to life? Was this God finished perhaps with the advent of the New Testament? Is Jesus Christ, as Marcion thought, the envoy of a different God, one more biddable and gentle? O God, how mean with you we are, and how pedantic!

The ways by which we set bounds to God's freedom are so many, and theologically so well justified, that we are convinced we are defending God's reliability, his credibility, his faithfulness, consistency, changelessness. What we don't understand is that God's faithfulness consists in being ever faithful to his newness, in ever creating anew, in doing new things and renewing old ones. If objective revelation has come to an end, his inexhaustible fertility has not. Only the Bible is 'bound up into a volume', from which nothing can be taken away, to which nothing can be added; not so, all that which from it is continually being raised up within the Church.

Above all, God claims this absolute freedom in the way he forms his saints, in the way he guides souls. It's been said that it isn't easy to live close to holy people and the deeper reason is precisely this: in them is manifest the sovereign freedom and creativity of God. 'Putting up' with this freedom, for anyone in authority, responsible for the common good, can become a veritable martyrdom. We shall be led into the dense darkness of the mystery, even at times of the absurd. God said these words to Jeremiah: 'If you find it exhausting to race against me on foot, how will you compete against horses? If you don't feel secure in a country at peace, how will you fare in the thickets of the Jordan?' (Jeremiah 12:5). Yes, here we are actually called to compete with horses, and with racehorses, although we are perhaps by nature sedentary; we are forced to make our way through 'the thickets', without being able to see anything, grasp anything, know where we're going, hemmed in by all sorts of fierce and dangerous beasts. But, deep down, we feel that taking this risk for God and with God (for God too runs a risk because of our freedom) is infinitely finer than walking along in safety, shielded from any surprise. The risk – the gravest in our lives – is not knowing whether we are walking towards God or in the diametrically opposite direction. Not to know this, at least by one's own 'reason', but only in another way, by faith, with the heart, through obedience and the Church's discernment which acts as a higher 'reason'. The essential thing is that this divine liberty should never become an excuse for living according to the flesh, and for this not to happen we must keep on dying a little to self and be constantly 'crucified with Christ on the cross'.

When we consider the great store God sets by our freedom, we ought to be ashamed at how little store we set by his. We ought to make it a point of honour to leave God free. Not only outside ourselves, in the Church, but above all inside ourselves, in our spiritual life. Free to give us joy and free to give us affliction, free to speak and free to be silent, free to reveal himself and free to hide. Virtually to restore to God that freedom he had over us, the instant, as it were, before he created us, when we were still no more than 'a thought in his heart' and he could have made us anything he pleased, without having to ask for or wait for our approval.

That was what Mary did. Saying: 'You see before you the Lord's servant, let it happen to me as you have said' (Luke 1:38), was, as Origen observes, as if she were saying to God: 'I am a wax tablet: let the Divine Scribe write what he will, do with me what he will, the Lord of all.'[118]

Let us say Charles de Foucauld's prayer about this together:

> Father,
> I surrender myself into your hands.
> Do with me what you will.
> Whatever you may do, I thank you;
> I am ready for all, I accept all.
> Only let your will be done in me
> And in all your creatures.
> I wish no more than this, O Lord.
> Into your hands I commend my soul.
> I offer it to you with all the love of my heart,
> For I love you, Lord, and so need to give myself,
> To surrender myself into your hands without reserve
> And with boundless confidence,
> For you are my Father.

26　It is the Spirit that gives life

Before we finally leave this uneven section of our journey behind us – in which we have witnessed the eclipse of the Living God in our culture – let us ask ourselves one question having bearing at once on the past and on the future: how has all this happened and how can it be prevented from happening again?

The answer can be summed up in just two words: the Holy Spirit. St Gregory of Nyssa writes: 'If we take the Holy Spirit away from God, what is left is no longer the Living God, but his corpse'.[19] So here we have the famous 'death of God' explained and here is something that anyone proposing to build a 'theology' on it would first of all have to get straight.

Jesus himself explains the reason why. 'It is the Spirit that gives life,' he says, 'the flesh has nothing to offer' (John 6:63). Applied to our case, this means: it is the Spirit that gives life to the idea of God and to research about him. Human reason, marked as it is by sin, is not enough on its own. In fact, it is almost useless since, even if it discovers that God exists, it isn't able subsequently to behave as it should by giving him glory and thanks.

Any believer who proposes to talk about God for whatever reason should remember that 'the secrets of God are unknown except to the Spirit of God' (1 Corinthians 2:11).

The Holy Spirit is the true 'vital setting', the *Sitz im Leben*, in which any genuinely Christian theology comes to birth and develops. Recent studies have shown that the very earliest meaning the Hebrew word *Ruah* (i.e. *Pneuma*, Spirit) had in the biblical world was not so much 'breath' or 'wind' but 'open space', in which the force of the wind manifests itself and where its presence may be perceived. This contributes something new to our understanding of the Holy Spirit, and this is moreover confirmed by the traditional way of speaking of him with an adverbial phrase of place: 'in' the Holy Spirit. He is that invisible space in which we can become aware of God's 'passing-by' and in which God appears as a living and active reality. Thus it is too with Christ. 'In the Holy Spirit' indicates that mysterious sphere in which, after his resurrection, one may enter into contact with Christ and experience his sanctifying activity. For Christ is alive 'in the Spirit' (cf. Romans 1:4; 1 Peter 3:18).

The great voltaic arc between God and us is not switched on therefore, and the sudden flash of light is not produced, except within that special magnetic field which, in matters of faith, consists of the Holy Spirit. He it is who in the human heart creates that state of grace, by which one day the great 'enlightening' can take place: the discovery that God exists, is real, and so 'to have our breath taken away'. In the course of a theological career or of a simple search for God, this produces a caesura and a leap, analogous to those we see in certain writers who, at times, in the course of a single composition, from prose suddenly break into verse and poetry, as though their thought had all at once taken wing and could only be expressed henceforth in song.

A theologian of our own day who has himself had this experience, puts it thus:

If theology is truly to be life-giving and in touch with reality, it needs to begin with an experience of God, not with philosophical reflection on absolute being. Theology in the future, as it did in the New Testament, must begin with the experience of the indwelling of the Holy Spirit in the Christian community. The doctrine and person of the Holy Spirit is not one doctrine among others, but a fundamental doctrine and reality in the Church. A renewal in the life of the Spirit, as we are beginning to experience, will affect not just one sector of church life or theology, but the whole.[120]

So how can anyone think of entering into contact with the Living God while leaving the Holy Spirit completely out of account? To those who would seek God somewhere else, only in the pages of books or in human theories, we should have to repeat what the angel said to the Holy Women: 'Why look among the dead for someone who is alive?' (Luke 24:5). On the Holy Spirit, says St Basil, depends 'familiarity with God'.[121] Depends, that is to say, whether God is familiar to us, or a stranger, whether we are sensitive or allergic to him.

Some people might object: Perhaps not enough is being said about the Spirit in the age in which we live. I reply: On the contrary, never has so much been said about Spirit. The very notion of 'Spirit' – variously conceived, as opposed to matter, world and nature – has indeed been carried in our own age to its point of maximum development: the concept of 'Absolute Spirit'. One might even define the notion of Spirit as a modern philosophical conquest, largely unknown to antiquity. So how can we explain this? It is because people have no longer been thinking of the 'Holy' Spirit, but of the 'spirit of history', or of the 'world-spirit', that is to say, the exact opposite of what Scripture regards as the 'Spirit of God' (cf. 1 Corinthians 2:12). But even when they have meant the Holy Spirit himself, the focus has usually been on the *idea* of him, rather than the *reality*.

The remedy is therefore to recover ever fuller contact with the reality, or better still the person, of the Holy Spirit. Let us not be satisfied with an updated pneumatology, that is to say, with a *theology* of the Spirit, but aspire to make him too a personal *experience*. If we think how, in practical terms, the Holy Spirit's absence produces a negative effect in our search for God and why it impedes us from attaining the Living God, we shall realize what importance this personal experience has, on the theological and rational plane too. The traditional proofs of the existence of God were refuted, as we have seen, because within them a cross-over from 'thought' to 'being' takes place, i.e. from the idea of a thing to its existence, which (as it was assumed at the time) belong to two different worlds. Only if God were the object of experience too, and not of thought alone, could his real existence be deduced. Which, it was thought, is manifestly impossible.

But this is the point. In people in whom the Holy Spirit is at work, no longer does God live only as an idea; he is reality, *the* reality. It is precisely in the Spirit that experience of God comes about; an experience doubtless imperfect, as a 'pledge' or 'first-fruits' of things to come (cf. Romans 8:23; 2 Corinthians 5:5), but a true experience, even though spiritual and not sensible.

In the Johannine writings, the Holy Spirit is called the 'Spirit of Truth' (John 14:17; 16:13) or simply 'truth' (1 John 5:6) where 'truth' stands for the reality of God as attained in himself and not in an image or intermediary. That is to say, it is the reality *known*, not *knowledge* about reality. Since therefore we must worship God 'in spirit and in truth', that is to say, not in the human manner, linked to places and shrines built with human hands, so we must know him 'in spirit and in truth', that is to say, in his own sphere not limited to purely human representations and ideas. In a word, knowing God by means of God.

For true believers (and particularly for mystics, in whom

this condition is realized to an eminent degree) God is no longer the object of speculation only, but of experience. And if it is true that not all of us can be mystics, it is nonetheless true that all of us can listen to and appreciate their witness, which is certainly worth as much as that of the philosophers.

Above all, in the Church we can all personally experience God in the Holy Spirit. In the New Testament we find two definitions referring to each other. The Holy Spirit is defined as 'the Spirit of the Living God' (2 Corinthians 3:3) and the Church is defined as 'the Church of the Living God' (1 Timothy 3:15). The Holy Spirit is thus defined in two senses: passive and active: since he proceeds from the Living God and since he leads to the Living God. And the Church too is defined thus in two senses: because she proceeds from the Living God as his creation, and because she leads humanity to the Living God. After Christ, she is in a quite peculiar, even if not exclusive, way that 'open space' of the Spirit, where it is possible for human beings to enter into contact with the mystery of the Living God.

That this may be truly so, especially in those places where theology is studied and future teachers of the faith are being trained, let us pray in the words of a famous hymn to the Holy Spirit:

> Come, O Creator Spirit, come
> and make within our heart your home,
> to us thy grace celestial give,
> who of thy breathing move and live . . .
> May we by thee the Father learn
> and know the Son and thee discern,
> who art of both; and thee adore
> in perfect faith for evermore.

27 Something majestic
to worship

Of the Holy Magi we read that, having left the city of Jerusalem behind with all the discussions of the doctors of the law and intrigues of Herod, with great joy they set out once more, following the star, found the Holy Child and 'bowing down, worshipped him' (Matthew 2:11). We ought to do something of the sort. Having got through the stormy section of our journey, for us too the moment has come to leave the turmoil of human opinions behind and resume our road towards the Living God so that we may worship him.

If indeed the sin making human beings 'inexcusable' is failing to acknowledge God as God, then its specific antidote is none other than worship, for only worship (being reserved exclusively to God) adequately attests that God is being acknowledged 'as God'. Worship is the highest expression of what the Apostle calls 'giving glory and saying thanks', that is to say, acknowledgment of and gratitude to God.

The New Testament, as we have already said, raised the word 'worship' to a dignity it had never known before. Each time, in the New Testament, someone is tempted to worship anyone who is not God in person, the immediate reaction is: 'Don't do it! God's the one to be worshipped' (cf. Revelation 19:10; 22:9; Acts 10:25–26; 14:12). Almost as though by doing the opposite, one would incur a mortal danger. The Church has perpetuated this teaching, making worship the act *par excellence* of devotion to God, *latria*, as distinct from *dulia* reserved for the saints, and *hyperdulia* reserved for the Blessed Virgin. Worship is therefore the unique religious act that can't be offered to anyone else in the entire universe, not even to Our Lady, but only to God. This is where its unique strength and dignity lie.

Now, in what does worship properly consist and how is it done? Worship can be prepared for by long reflection but ends with an intuition and, like every intuition, this does not last long. It is like a flash of light in the dark. But of a special light, not so much the light of truth as the light of reality. It is a perception of the greatness, majesty, beauty and at the same time the goodness of God and of God's presence, which takes one's breath away. It is a sort of shipwreck in the boundless, bottomless ocean of the majesty of God. But 'shipwreck is sweet in this sea'.[122]

One expression of worship, more efficacious than any words, is silence. For it says of itself that the reality is altogether beyond any words. Loudly through the Bible rings the summons: 'Let the whole earth be silent before him!' (Habakkuk 2:20) and: 'Silence in the presence of the Lord God!' (Zephaniah 1:7). When 'the senses are enfolded in a limitless silence and with the help of the silence our memories grow dim,' then worship is all there's left to do.

According to some authorities, the Latin word for worship, *adorare*, denotes the gesture of putting one's hand over one's mouth as though to enforce silence. If this is so, Job's was a gesture of worship when, having had his person-to-person debate with the Almighty, at the end of his vicissitudes he says: 'My words have been frivolous: what can I reply? I had better lay my hand over my mouth' (Job 40:4). In this sense, the psalm verse taken into the liturgy says in the Hebrew text: 'For you silence is praise', *Tibi silentium laus*! (cf. Psalm 65:2, Massoretic text). Worship, according to St Gregory Nazianzen's wonderful expression quoted earlier, means raising 'a silent hymn' to God. As, when we gradually climb into the mountain heights the air becomes rarer, so as we gradually draw nearer to God, our words become briefer until they finally become completely mute, and we are united in silence to the Ineffable.[123]

If we really need to say something to 'close' our mind and prevent it from wandering onto other subjects, it's best to do this with the shortest word there is: Amen, Yes. For to worship is to consent. It is to let God be God. It is to say yes to God as God, and to ourselves as God's creatures. It is therefore the remedy for despair, for this consists, as we have seen, precisely in a 'desperate not-wishing to be what we are', that is to say, dependent on God.

Worship therefore requires that we should bow down and shut up. But is such behaviour worthy of a human being? Isn't this humiliating for us, detracting from our dignity? On the contrary, is it really worthy of God? What sort of God is he if he needs his creatures to bow down to him in silence? Is God perhaps like one of those Eastern monarchs who invented a cult of themselves? It is useless to deny it: worship does indeed entail for creatures an element of radical humiliation, of making oneself small, of surrendering. It was precisely this, as we saw, that held the pagans back from worshipping God as God. Worship always entails an element of sacrifice, of giving something up. This is precisely what attests that God is God and that nothing and no one has the right to exist before him, save by his grace. With worship we give up, we sacrifice our very self, our own glory, our own self-sufficiency. But this is a false and inconsistent glory, and for us to get shot of it is a liberation.

By worshipping, we liberate the truth which before was 'the prisoner of unrighteousness'. We become genuine, in the deepest meaning of the word. In worship, we anticipate the return of all things to God. We surrender ourselves to the meaning and flow of existence. As water finds its peace in gliding towards the sea, and the bird its joy in following the course of the wind, so the worshipper in worshipping. Worshipping God is not therefore so much a duty or an obligation as a privilege, even a need. We need something majestic to love and worship! We are made for this. So God is not the one who needs to be worshipped, we are the ones who need to do it; and Nietzsche was completely off the track when he defined the biblical God as 'that oriental greedy for honours on his heavenly throne'.[124] (Many people, believers and theologians included, invoke this thinker all too lightly.)

How different his language from that of Kierkegaard the believer:

> Man, whose body stands upright towards the sky, is a being that worships. His stature is the sign that marks him out, but the ability to bow down in worship is an even higher characteristic. The supreme glory consists in being nothing and worshipping. Some people consider his resemblance to God lies in the power to rule. But it is not by ruling as God that man is like God. The resemblance is only to be found at the heart of an infinite difference. As I understand it, man and God resemble each other in a relationship not directly but inversely proportional: for there to be any resemblance, God needs to become the eternal and omnipresent object of worship, and man needs to become a creature incessantly worshipping. If man claims to make himself like God by ruling, he forgets God and, once God has disappeared, plays the sovereign in his absence. This is just paganism: man's life in God's absence.[125]

Worship however must be free. What makes worship worthy of God and at the same time worthy of the human being is freedom, understood not only negatively as absence of constraint, but also positively as joyous outburst, spontaneous gift of the creature, as like this we express our joy at not ourselves being God, at having a God above ourselves to worship, to admire, to celebrate.

For God too, the value of worship lies in freedom. 'I myself am free,' says God,

> and I have created man in my own image and likeness . . . This creature's freedom is the loveliest reflection in the world of the Creator's freedom . . . When you have once experienced what it is to be loved freely, subjugation loses its savour. Once you have known what it's like to be loved by free men, the prostrations of slaves mean nothing to you.[126]

Let us pray with the words and sentiments of the Christian philosopher whom we have just quoted:

> Even if, supposing that you, God, were not love but only infinite, detached majesty, I could not help loving you. I need something majestic to love. In my soul there is a need for a majesty that I could never, never grow weary of worshipping.[127]

28   In the cleft of the rock

At this point we should take another look at the passage from St
Paul from which we set out, for we do not want to run the risk of
suggesting a different remedy for lack of worship from the one
propounded by the Word of God, since it would be a wrong one.
What was the remedy the Apostle suggested for the sin of the
pagans? Perhaps that of being converted and glorifying God as of
old before their minds had been darkened? Or that of contemplating the stars and other works of creation once more but more
attentively, and in them discovering God and so worshipping
him? No good! The remedy lies ahead, not behind. It is the one
the Apostle is to tell us about, further on in his letter. The real
remedy lies not so much in the sphere of creation as in the sphere
of redemption. St Paul has more to say about the worship (*latria*)
of God in the twelfth chapter of the letter, that is, only after
presenting the work of Christ and the Holy Spirit. The new
worship will indeed be a worship offered 'by the Spirit of God'
(Philippians 3:3), no longer only with the intellect as heretofore.

The consequence is that now worship must come through

Christ: 'Glory to him in the Church and in Christ Jesus' (Ephesians 3:21). The very quality of worship is changed. We are talking about something new and different from any type of worship to be found in other religious systems. Christ the Man-God is the perfect glory and perfect thanksgiving to the Father. To worship God henceforth means to be united, in the Spirit, to Jesus Christ, who is the perfect worshipper of the Father, 'the great mystery of our religion' (1 Timothy 3:16), who has put an end to all ungodliness. This is worship offered by one who is God and human being in the same person, who therefore bridges the ontological gulf existing between worshipper and worshipped. At last we have a worship 'worthy of God'.

Jesus and the Holy Spirit too, being divine persons, are worshipped. By substituting the word 'worship' for the word 'prayer', we can say with St Augustine:

> Our Lord Jesus Christ, the Son of God, is he who worships
> for us, who worships in us and who is worshipped by us. He
> worships for us as our Priest, he worships in us as our Head,
> and is worshipped by us as our God.[128]

We have seen how in the New Testament, when anyone tries to worship an angel or an apostle, the immediate reaction of the party concerned is to cry out: 'Don't do it!' When however the Canaanite woman, the man born blind, the apostles themselves, do the same thing to the earthly Jesus, he never protests and says: 'Don't do it!' and nor do the apostles, though knowing that God alone should be worshipped (cf. Matthew 4:10), feel that such expressions of worship need to be corrected. A remarkable thing, which constitutes an unintentional proof – and an all the more convincing one for that – of the Early Church's faith in the divinity of Christ.

Christian worship is therefore trinitarian. It is this in its direction and in its dynamism, since it is worship offered 'to the Father, through the Son, in the Holy Spirit'; and it is this in its end or object, since it is worship offered 'to the Father, to the Son and to the Holy Spirit' together.

All this means that when, moved inwardly by grace, we feel the need arise in us to worship, and we realize that words are not enough, bowing down to the ground is not enough, that not even silence is sufficient, that all is insipid and that all is infinitely too little, we have an escape route from this feeling of helplessness. We can, by faith, ask the Holy Spirit (which is just what he expects!) to unite us to Jesus Christ and thus, united to him, worship the Father. For instance making use of the words in the liturgy of the Mass, which express all this to perfection:

> Through Christ, with Christ, in Christ, in the unity of the
> Holy Spirit, all glory and honour is yours, almighty Father,
> for ever and ever.

This is the worship 'in spirit and in truth' of which Jesus spoke in his conversation with the Samaritan woman, which constitutes the Magna Carta of Christian worship:

> Believe me, woman, the hour is coming when you will
> worship the Father neither on this mountain nor in
> Jerusalem. You worship what you do not know; we worship
> what we do know; for salvation comes from the Jews. But
> the hour is coming – indeed is already here – when true
> worshippers will worship the Father in spirit and in truth;
> this is the kind of worshipper the Father seeks. God is spirit,
> and those who worship him must worship him in spirit and
> in truth (John 4:21–24).

The words 'spirit and truth' certainly have various levels of meaning here, ranging from those more subjective ones to do with our dispositions (interiority, sincerity, freedom), to other more objective ones connected with realities outside ourselves. The highest level of all, among those objective meanings, is the one in which 'spirit' means the Holy Spirit and 'truth' means the Truth, that is, Christ himself.

The 'spirit and the truth' is what Christ brought down to earth: it is the new possibility created by his coming. In the Book of Exodus we read that on Sinai God showed Moses a cleft in the rock where he could hide and so be able to gaze on God's glory without dying (cf. Exodus 33:21). Commenting on this passage, St Basil writes:

> What, for us Christians, is that cleft today, that place in which we can take refuge to gaze on and worship God? It is the Holy Spirit. From whom did we learn this? From the Lord himself, who said, 'The true worshippers will worship the Father in Spirit and truth'![129]

If therefore in one sense we are temples of the Holy Spirit (cf. 1 Corinthians 6:19), in another it is the Holy Spirit who is our temple. We are his human temple, he is our divine temple.

What perspectives, what beauty, what power, what attractiveness all this confers on the ideal of Christian worship! Who in the seething maelstrom of the world does not feel the need from time to time to hide in the spiritual cleft to gaze at God and worship him, like Moses? There is a place, a space, a sort of invisible niche within us, ever ready to welcome us, wherever we are, whatever we are doing. In it we can worship the Father in Spirit and truth. In our times, the Holy Spirit is attracting more and more souls into that mysterious cleft of his which (as we have seen) some have called 'the depths of the soul'. The thought allows them no peace, that the Father, from the heavens, 'is seeking such worshippers', is waiting for them, wants them; he scans the earth in search of them. He seeks them to fill them with himself, to sate them 'at the torrent of his delights' (Psalm 36:8).

One of the most wonderful gifts that the Holy Spirit, redis-covered in our own times, bestows on the Church is this: that he reveals the Living God to us and prompts us to worship him. The so-called Movement for Charismatic Renewal in the Catholic Church indeed began with a powerful experience of the presence of the Living God, produced by the Holy Spirit. The people taking part in the first retreat, when these experiences began, were in the chapel one evening before the Blessed Sacrament when suddenly an extraordinary thing happened, which one of them later described as follows:

> Fear of the Lord welled up within us; a fearful awe kept us from looking up. He was personally present and we feared being loved too much. We worshipped him, knowing for the first time the meaning of worship. We knew a burning experience of the terrible reality and presence of the Lord that has since caused us to understand at first hand the metaphors of Yahweh on Mount Sinai as it rumbles and explodes with the fire of his Being, and the experience of Isaiah 6:1–5, and the statement that our God is a consuming fire. This holy fear was somehow the same as love or evoked love as we really beheld him. He was altogether lovely and beautiful, yet we saw no visual image. It was as though the splendorous, brilliant, personal God had come into the room and filled both it and us.[130]

Simultaneous presence of majesty and sweetness in God, of awe and love in those who behold him: the man who described that moment thus didn't know that he was perfectly summing up the essential traits of the Living God of the Bible which we mentioned at the outset.

Let us pray with the Church:

> All-powerful and ever-living God,
> you have no need of our praise,
> yet our desire to praise you
> is itself your gift;
> our prayer of thanksgiving
> adds nothing to your greatness
> but makes us grow in your grace.
> Through Christ our Lord.[131]

29   Fear God and glorify him!

I have just mentioned a few opportunities and forms that personal, silent worship may take. But this is not the only possible way. There is also an external worship, composed of fixed gestures and words, in which we may join an ampler, liturgical worship, the very breath of the Church. For those of us who feel the need, a new desire to worship, born in our heart, the liturgy and praxis of the Church offer a whole range of opportunities, made up of gestures and words, to accompany us in this task. From the moment we wake up in the morning until we go to bed at night. At daybreak, as soon as we get up, we begin the Divine Office, and lo and behold, in the *Invitatory* we forthwith find one of the most beautiful exhortations to worship in the whole Bible:

> Come, let us bow low and do reverence,
> kneel before the Lord who made us . . . (Psalm 95:6).

At Holy Mass, in the *Gloria* we say: 'We praise you, we bless you, we worship you, we glorify you, we give you thanks for your great glory.' We worship you and we give you thanks, not for some favour you bestow on us, but for your great glory. Simply because you are God, simply because you exist. Purest of sentiments! To give glory and thanks to God 'as is due to God'. Then the *Trisagion*: 'Holy, holy, holy, Lord God of hosts . . . ' which has always been one of the most exalted forms of worship for the majesty of God, since the prophet Isaiah heard it ring out from the seraphim in heaven.

During the day, each genuflexion we make is an opportunity for reviving this spirit of worship. A genuflexion well done is in itself a complete act of worship. In the Greek language, in which the New Testament was written, to worship (*proskyneo*) properly means to bow to the ground.

But worship is not limited to these instants; it is a state of mind, an intention of heart, which one may harbour whatever one is doing. When it is present, it transforms every prayer and every act into worship; it makes every minute service-time. We each of us have our own way of access, means all our own to help us put ourselves in the presence of the Living God and enter into a state of worship, a secret path as it were known only to ourselves. It may be words from the Bible that mean a lot to us ('My soul is athirst for God, the Living God!', 'My soul cleaves to you!' . . .), or it may be an inward or external image, an ikon such as that of the Trinity by Rublev, or the memory of a moment of grace and light experienced in the past.

The sense of the worship of God needs to be restored to honour in our Western culture and spirituality. Above all, in our own lives of personal piety. In this field, worship reveals itself to be a formidable weapon at our disposal in the spiritual combat. What happens if – in moments of strong temptation or of inner rebellion, when the spirit of revolt stirs in the camp of the old Adam – I take that kind of battle-cry literally, the one I have just mentioned: 'Come, let us bow low and do reverence . . . ' and actually kneel down before a crucifix? What happens is that I put my pride, my sensuality, in a word, my sin, 'on its knees before the Lord my maker'. I set God's foes 'as a footstool beneath his feet'. I anticipate the Last Judgment when 'every knee shall bow before him' (cf. Romans 14:11), when every evil will be recognized as such and God will be declared 'right in his judgment' (cf. Psalm 50:6). This is the best way of 'surprising' the Enemy, the Enemy of God and of me, and of forcing him to surrender. After that, sin, even if present, no longer 'reigns' in me; it is forced to abdicate. The sanctifying power of worship!

Besides in the life of personal piety, worship next needs to be restored to honour in the liturgy, in the way of practising theology and exegesis, and above all in evangelization. The best evangelization is that which starts with worship and leads to worship. A moment with which, according to historians, the first systematic evangelization of Europe begins after the so-called barbarian invasions, was the baptism of Clovis, King of the Franks. This took place at Rheims on Christmas Eve in the years 498 or 499 at the hands of the bishop, St Remi. The words the holy bishop uttered on this occasion are still famous: 'Bow your head humbly, Sicambrian! Worship what you have burnt and burn what you have worshipped!'[132] (The Sicambrians were a very proud and warlike people who had settled astride the borders of present-day France and Germany, in the very heart of Europe.)

It is significant that at the start of the evangelization of Europe we should find these two commands: 'Bow your head humbly and worship!' We need someone with the authority and holiness of St Remi, St Boniface, St Gall, St Columba and the other great pioneers of evangelization of old, to repeat these same commands today. Worship doesn't serve only to prepare the way for evangelization, it actually is evangelization. A female missionary, who has worked for many years in a very poor country in Africa, recently wrote to me as follows:

We are called to respond to a basic human need, to the
deep need for God, to the thirst for the Absolute, to teach
the road to God, to teach people how to pray. This, you see,
is why the Muslims make so many converts in these parts:
they teach them immediately, and in a simple way, to
worship God.

Christians, as we know, have a very different content to put into
their worship but need to learn anew how to do it, since they have
often lost the feel of it.

We can learn much too, in this respect, from our Jewish
brothers, at least from those among them who practise their religion. How devout and salutary, the custom that's observed in
Jewish religious literature, such as the *Talmud* and other ancient
writings, never to name the Lord (*Adonai* in their language)
without forthwith interpolating the words: 'Blessed be he!
Blessed be he!', as though fearing to read on too hastily and inat-
tentively and so show lack of reverence for God.

In the Book of Revelation we read of an angel who, flying
through the heavens, cried out in a great voice to the inhabitants
of earth: 'Fear God and glorify him . . . Worship the maker of
heaven and earth' (Revelation 14:7). Would to God, the
Christian Churches of Europe and the West, setting aside their
ancient divisions and quarrels (which have little or nothing to do
with God's glory), would learn in brotherly concord to echo that
angelic voice on earth. For 'it is a dreadful thing to fall into the
hands of the Living God' (Hebrews 10:31). To fall into them as
his enemies, or simply from being too carefree.

Let us pray in the words of a German Protestant poet and mystic
who lifted up his voice in the midst of the Enlightenment to
remind the world of the duty to worship:

God is present here,
>   let us come and worship!
With holy reverence,
>   let us come into his presence.
God is here in the midst,
>   let all keep silent in us
and the depths of the heart
>   bow down before him.
Let whoever knows him,
>   whoever says his name,
turn his eyes to the ground
>   and turn his heart back to him.[133]

30 Desire for God

There is another attitude, besides worship, that we can cultivate in our relationship with the Living God, and that is desire. I am well aware that faith, hope and charity are the three essential modes by which we relate to God and establish a kind of 'spiritual contact' with him. But the importance and beauty of desire lie precisely in the fact that desire is the result and synthesis of these three things: faith, hope and charity. Desire is like a single flame burning on a tripod. It is the essential implication of the three theological virtues, almost the detector of their presence and activity.

To know what desire for God is, first of all we have to know what desire is. There are two distinct components in desire: one negative, one positive. The Latin word from which ours is derived points up the negative component; the Greek word, used in the New Testament, the positive. In the language of divination as practised by the Romans, *desiderare* meant to note an absence of stars (*sidera*) needed for taking the omens. From this, in common speech, the term came to mean 'to feel the lack of something'.

The corresponding Greek term, *potheo*, originally means the movement of stretching out, reaching out towards something, longing for, yearning for. The accent falls more on the positive and dynamic aspect of desire. For the Stoics, desire was a spiritual aspiration based on a conscious decision of the will, guided by reason. The soul, by means of desire, stretched out, dilated itself in time, impatient to obtain what it yearned for. This is the sense the word has in the biblical passage where it says that in this life we are like exiles who 'long' (*epipotheo*) for their eternal home (cf. 2 Corinthians 5:2). (The distinction between the two senses, negative and positive, of desiring corresponds, as we see, more or less to the one in modern English between the two verbs *to miss* and *to long for*.)

These elements of meaning are both present, turn and turn about, in the Bible, when desire for God is the subject:

> As a deer yearns for running streams,
> so my soul yearns for you, my God (Psalm 42:1).

Here desire is expressed in the positive, with the image of the deer which, hearing the babbling of a brook, rushes headlong down the crags to drink. (Anyone who has followed the course of the Wadi el-Kelt cutting across the wilderness of Judaea from Jerusalem towards Jericho would know what the psalmist has in mind.) But this verse is immediately followed by these other words:

> My soul is athirst for God,
> the Living God,

which express the same desire in the negative, as a feeling of thirst, i.e. lack of God.

With these few notions about desire in general, let us now

raise ourselves to specific consideration of desire for God, which is the deepest of the human heart's desires, even though so often ignored. As the night, says a fine poem by Tagore, hides in its darkness the desire it has for light, and as the storm secretly seeks peace in the calm that will follow its fury, so in the unconscious depths of the human heart the cry resounds: 'I desire You, only You!'[134]

The desire for God is spoken of in two different contexts and two different ways. First of all, there is the 'natural desire for God' as philosophical and theological concept (which serves as point of departure for St Augustine and St Thomas for one of the famous proofs of God's existence), and there is the desire for God, known to those souls in love with him, which doesn't have proof of God but his conquest as its aim, and isn't a concept but a feeling. Between the two exists the same difference as between a scientific description of the phenomenon of thirst, and the actual thirst of someone who has been walking for hours under the desert sun. Someone concerned with the natural desire for God may very well never have personally experienced this kind of desire in his soul; just as, vice versa, someone who has experienced 'live' this desire may very well never have reflected on it as a way of deducing that God exists. And yet, between the two desires for God – the one natural and the other supernatural – there is no contradiction: for the second presupposes the first and is founded on it, precisely as grace presupposes nature.

There would be so much to be said even about the natural desire for God. It, it has been said, is 'that which is deepest in us, most essential and most exalted in the human being'; it is 'the very foundation of Christian anthropology' according to de Lubac. Yet we wonder whether this natural desire for God is still to be found in secularized, twentieth-century people. Does the Augustinian argument of the 'unquiet heart' still apply? It seems to me that in one part of modern culture the positive element of this desire has disappeared, but that the negative one is still in place. The yearning has gone, the stretching out to God in faith and prayer; only the void left by his disappearance now remains. The sense of his loss remains, that is to say, that yearning for God which someone has called 'the yearning for the totally other'.[135]

But we for our part are mainly interested in the other type of desire for God, the supernatural one manifestly conjoined with faith, hope and charity. It is the motor, or driving force, of the spiritual life. This it is that gives the impetus needed for overcoming difficulties. Nothing worthwhile can be done without desire. We don't become saints without a strong desire to become so. We are only drawn nearer to God by our soul's desires, not by our feet!

St Augustine has sometimes been described as the doctor of the desire for God, owing to the importance he attaches to this theme and the accents in which he speaks of it. 'Desire', he says,

> is the inmost recess of the heart. The more desire dilates our heart, the more able we become to welcome God.
>
> The life of a good Christian is just one holy desire . . . By desire, you dilate yourself, so that you can be filled when you reach the vision . . . By this waiting, God increases our desire, with desire he enlarges our soul, and by dilating it makes it able to hold more. Let us live then, brothers, by desire, since we must be filled.

Prayer itself is lively when desire is lively, flowing within us:

> Your desire is your prayer; if desire is continual, prayer is continual . . . If you do not mean to stop praying, never stop desiring.
>
> Sustained prayer consists in raising a continuous and devout impulse of the heart to him, whom we invoke.[136]

'We,' says a prayer in the liturgy, 'shine in God's eyes because of our desire for him.'[137] As though God were to look down from heaven and see brighter or less bright points of light on earth, depending on the intensity of our desire for him.

Mystical literature is full of this theme of the desire for God. 'Longing love', the anonymous medieval author calls it. We have met him already. 'So pay attention', he says,

> to the marvellous work of grace within your soul. It always stirs suddenly, unexpectedly, rapidly, springing up to God like sparks from the coal . . . Strike hard at that thick cloud of unknowing with a sharp dart of longing love. And whatever happens, don't give up.[138]

As therefore the sea never wearies night and day of driving its waves, now mighty, now calm, towards the shore, so we must never grow weary of driving these silent impulses of the heart towards God. And if, during this work, your mind in its impertinence should try to interrupt with questions such as: 'What is God and how can I think about him?' answer: 'I know nothing and, at this moment, I want to know nothing. It's more important to love God than to think about him.'

Now, the desire for God is not only an important factor in the ascetical and spiritual life, but also in preaching. I have to confess that sometimes I have complained a bit to God, saying: 'Lord, if you wish me in my preaching to talk to other people about humility, charity, prayer, why don't you grant me a little of these things, of which I'm so short?' And the answer I have sensed within me has been: 'What are the things people talk about most enthusiastically: what they already possess, or what they desire?' 'What they desire,' I hastily replied, and suddenly grasped that I must have all my life been always talking about what I don't possess but do desire. I try at least to follow the advice an ancient Father used to give to people who had to speak and write about spiritual things which they had not yet acquired in life: 'Talk of them as one who belongs to the disciple-class and not as one with authority, having first humbled your soul and made yourself smaller than your listener.'[139]

Let us pray, we too reciting the 'song of Adam driven from Paradise', beloved of many an Orthodox ascetic:

My soul yearns for you, O Lord, and with tears I seek you. Look on my affliction and lighten my darkness, so that my soul may rejoice. How can I forget you? Your serene and gentle gaze allured my soul and gladdened my spirit in Paradise where I used to see your face.[140]

31   Your name, your memory
      are all our soul desires

One of the differences between the natural and supernatural desire for God is that the former is innate, but the latter acquired. So this desire needs to be acquired. How? This too 'by subtraction'. In sculpture, you need to chip away the useless bits of stone to let the projected work of art gradually emerge. Just so, we have to chip away our useless desires, earthly desires, so that desire for God can grow stronger.

There is a big difference between earthly desires and desire for God. For the former do not always come true, however strong they may be; the latter always comes true, since God never lets any desire for him go unfulfilled. Furthermore, the former, once realized, give rise to satiety and dissatisfaction; while the latter when realized generates even greater hunger and thirst for God: 'They who drink of me will thirst for more' (Ecclesiasticus 24:21).

But why then are earthly desires so much more lively and powerful in us and so much more readily beguiling than desire for God? It is because they present us more immediate objects, which seize directly on the senses and the will-to-pleasure inherent in our nature. The sun is much larger than the earth and the force of attraction of its mass is such that it holds incredibly distant planets and their satellites captive; yes, we too are attracted to the sun, but our feet are still stuck fast to the earth. This, being nearer, is able to neutralize the sun's attraction. And so it is, between desire for God and desire for earthly things and earthly pleasures.

We must aspire to that point where in all sincerity we can exclaim with the psalmist: 'With you, I lack nothing on earth' (Psalm 73:25). That point had been reached by the martyr St Ignatius of Antioch, who could say: 'All my lust has been crucified and the fire of earthly desire is no more within me. Only a living water speaks within me, saying: "Come to the Father!"'[141] At first sight, the two things – lust and desire – seem very close to one another, so close indeed that sometimes the Bible uses the same word for both. But in fact there is an abyss between them. Desire takes you out of yourself, lust draws to you; desire surrenders, lust keeps back.

Of course, the Christian spiritual life is no stranger to the struggle to extinguish the desires, the struggle for impassivity or, as the masters of Christian spirituality prefer to say, for 'holy indifference'. But there is a big difference between this and analogous ideals outside Christianity. In Christianity the extinction of desire is not an end in itself; the motive for it isn't the negative one 'of halting the wheel of pain'. The extinguishing of the desires has to serve for the strengthening of that unique desire which, satisfied, satisfies absolutely and for ever. This is not with a view to Nothingness, but the All.

But what counts more for the Christian than the ascetic way of mortifying earthly desires, is the positive way, I mean, the Holy Spirit. He it is who raises the desire for God in the heart. 'He who can see into all hearts (that is, God) knows what the Spirit's desires are' (Romans 8:27). The Holy Spirit it is who breathes within us, that is to say, who makes us breathe, with inexpressible groanings. He it is who creates the true, deep yearning for God. Speaking of that yearning and that sighing after the heavenly fatherland which characterizes our condition as wayfarers, the Apostle concludes: 'God has given us the Spirit as a pledge' (2 Corinthians 5:5). We understand then why St Bonaventure could write the lapidary and very allusive words we find at the end of his book *The Soul's Journey into God*:

> This most secret and mystical wisdom no one can know
> except him who receives it, no one receives it except him who
> desires it, and no one desires it except him who is inflamed in
> his very marrow by the fire of the Holy Spirit, whom Christ
> sent into the world.[142]

There are various means by which we can express in prayer to God the desire that we have for him. But the best is offered us by the Bible itself, particularly the psalms. A little while ago I mentioned Psalm 42, which speaks of the deer that pants for the water-brooks. But that psalm is not the only one. Psalm 63 also expresses the desire for God negatively and positively, that is to say, as a feeling of his absence and as a reaching out towards him:

> God, you are my God, I pine for you;
> my heart thirsts for you,
> my body longs for you,
> as a land parched, dreary and waterless.

Yet another psalm speaks of someone who 'raises' his soul to God (Psalm 25:1), and the prophet Isaiah exclaims on behalf of all his nation: 'Lord, we set our hopes in you; your name, your memory are all our soul desires' (Isaiah 26:8). Any one of these expressions can, if we wish, become a kind of ejaculatory prayer to be repeated over and over again within us to rekindle the flame of desire.

Let us too, having reached the end of our journey, address ourselves to God in the fervent prayer by St Augustine, who has been our guide so often in the course of it:

> Late have I loved you, Beauty so ancient and so new.
> Late have I loved you.
> In my ugliness
> I plunged into the beauties that you have made.
> You were with me, but I was not with you.
> You called me, you cried out, you shattered my deafness.
> You blazed forth, you shone, you scattered my blindness.
> You breathed perfume, I drew in my breath, now I pant for you.
> I tasted and now I am hungry and thirsty for you.
> You touched me and now I burn with desire for your peace.[143]

EPILOGUE
I shall be your God

And so, dear sisters and brothers, we have reached the end of our journey to Sinai. But, for us too, let the end of the book not be the end of our quest. Rather, let it be the beginning. When all voices and all words fall silent, it is easier in that silence to encounter the Living God in person. Like the *idea*, the *book* too can all too easily become a screen, act as a veil, rather than as a means to the Living God. (Many a time in the course of these pages I have warned you of this danger and, without realizing, have perhaps made the same mistake as the painter who was more preoccupied with his king's portrait than with his king. If this is so, I ask pardon of God and you.) And so, quoting an author whom we have met before in the course of these pages, I say:

> Friend, it is now enough. Would'st thou read more, go hence, become thyself the Writing and thyself the Sense.[144]

But we can't say goodbye and come down from our Sinai again, without first having made a concrete gesture to set, as it were, a seal on our spiritual journey. Sinai is the mountain of theophany, but of the covenant too. On it God gave Moses the tablets of the Law and struck that covenant which Jesus was later to transform by his blood into a new and everlasting one.

The act we ought to perform therefore is that of renewing our covenant with God, choosing him once again, wittingly and definitively, as the only God in our life. All we have to do is to gather all our being into a unity: body, soul, brain, will, emotions, desires, past, present and future, and with all the determination of which we are capable, supported by the Spirit who 'comes to the help of our weakness', pronounce, or rather cry out, we too, our total and irreversible: 'I want God!'

Together with God, to welcome whatever his will may be, expressed in the commandments and in Jesus's Gospel, by saying, like the people on Sinai: 'We shall do everything the Lord has said; we shall obey' (Exodus 24:7). Let us make ours for now this beautiful prayer which our Protestant brothers of the Methodist tradition recite at the end of the service they actually have for renewing the covenant:

> I am no longer my own, but yours. Put me to what you will, rank me with whom you will; put me to doing, put me to suffering; let me be employed for you or laid aside for you, exalted for you or brought low for you; let me be full, let me be empty; let me have all things, let me have nothing; I freely and heartily yield all things to your pleasure and disposal.[145]

The classic covenantal formula is 'You will be my people and I shall be your God' (Ezekiel 36:28). Our own happiness lies in discovering the force of that possessive adjective 'your'. God is ours! The Living God whom, groping our way, we have tried to track down in these pages, is ours, belongs to us! He is more 'mine' by far than are the house I live in, the woman I'm married to, the children I've given birth to, my own body, my very life. 'Closer to me than my very self.'[146]

This is the most perfect form of possession, since it is intrinsic, not extrinsic: a possessing of the One who possesses us. We really possess something or some person, if we can 'enjoy' this, that is to say, dispose of this, derive benefit from this. And that is what we are destined for: 'to enjoy God' (*frui Deo*) for ever.

Who can explain this mystery of grace? God 'is' God, but the creature 'has' God. The difference between us and God is reduced, we might say, to the difference there is between being and having. No one except God can say: 'I am God!' but all of us can say, if we want him: 'I have God!' God is mine. 'O God, you are *my* God!' (Psalm 63:1).

In one sense we are better off than God. God hasn't got a God above him to admire, to be proud of, to complain to. We have! (On more careful consideration we realize that what I have said is not quite accurate, for God too has someone to love, to admire, to be cheered up by and to fill his loneliness, for the Living God is one, but also three: the Father has the Son, the Son has the Father, and both of them have the Holy Spirit.) This is the 'creaturely' joy, the joy those people deprive themselves of, who do not want to have a God but to be God themselves.

Having heard God calling him on Sinai with the words: 'Climb up to me!', the moment came when Moses heard a new command: 'Go down! Then come back bringing Aaron with you' (Exodus 19:24). That same command is now addressed to us. We must 'tell' about the Living God and make other people want to climb up Sinai. Our Aaron, with whom to begin, might be the man or woman who lives next door, friends, our fellow worker, someone God puts in our way. The first time we climb Sinai, we go it alone, the second time with someone else; no longer as just a climber but as a guide.

It is written that 'when Moses came down from Mount

Sinai, he did not know that the skin of his face was radiant'
(Exodus 34:29). He didn't know it but other people did, and it
was precisely this mysterious light on Moses's face and in his eyes
that spoke from now on to the Israelites of the Living God who
was journeying in their midst. It was a shadow and an image, in
anticipation of the divine glory which was to blaze on another
face – Christ's (cf. 2 Corinthians 4:6).

Now, as happens when we go our separate ways at the end
of a group pilgrimage which has given rise to deep fellowship and
friendship among those taking part, we too exchange the simple
salutation, which in this case is literally true: 'Adieu!' Until we
meet again before God, the Living God, never to part again for all
eternity. There we shall have no need of books or words. 'Now
we see only reflections in a mirror, mere riddles, but then we shall
be seeing face to face' (1 Corinthians 13:12).

Let us end with the prayer the Church addresses to God on the
feast of the Epiphany:

> Grant, we beseech you, Lord,
> that we who know you now by faith,
> may be mercifully brought to see your glorious majesty,
> one day, face to face.
> Through Christ our Lord. Amen.

Notes

1 St Augustine, *Confessions*, I, 1.

2 Cf. Archimandrite Sophrony, *The Monk of Mount Athos, Staretz Silouan*, tr. Edmonds, London, Mowbrays, 1973, p. 30.

3 Angelus Silesius, *Cherubinischer Wandersmann*, II, 83.

4 '*Zu den Sachen selbst*' is the programme of the phenomenological school of Husserl.

5 St Thomas Aquinas, *Summa Theologiae*, II–IIae, q. 1, 2, 2.

6 J-P. Sartre, *La nausée*, in *Oeuvres romanesques*, Paris, Gallimard, p. 105f.

7 Cf. G. von Rad, *Theologie des Alten Testaments*, I, Monaco, 1966, p. 194.

8 St Anselm, *Proslogion*, 1, in *Opera Omnia* I, Edinburgh, 1946, p. 100.

9 St Augustine, *De Trinitate*, VI, 10, 11.

10 St Gregory of Nyssa, *In Canticum Canticorum* XI, 5, 2 (PG 44, 1001).

11 Cf. Dante Alighieri, *Paradiso*, XXXIII, vv. 59–63.

12 Rudolf Otto, *The Idea of the Holy*, OUP reprint, 1968, p. 7.

13 St Augustine, *Sermo* 223A, 5 (Misc. Agost. I, pp. 15f).

14 Ibid., *Enarrationes in Psalmos*, 85, 12 (CCL 39, p. 1186); *Confessions*, X, 6.

15 Anon., *The Cloud of Unknowing*, 7, ed. Backhouse, London, Hodder & Stoughton, 1985, p. 30.

16 H. de Lubac, *Histoire et Esprit*, chapter 5, Paris, Aubier, 1950.

17 St Augustine, *De Trinitate*, XV, 28, 51.

18 Ibid., *De Civitate Dei*, IX, 15, 2.

19 Ibid., *De Trinitate*, VI, 10, 10.

20 Roman Missal, *Eucharistic Prayer* IV.

21 Dame Julian of Norwich, *Revelations*, chapter 52.

22 St Augustine, *Confessions*, X, 20.

23 Dante, *Purgatorio*, XXVII, 115f.

24 J.W. von Goethe, *Faust*, Part II, Act V, lines 11581–7.

25 Roman Missal, *Collect for 21st Sunday in Ordinary Time*.

26 St Ambrose, *De Paradiso*, 14, 18 (PL 14, 308).

27 St Cyril of Jerusalem, *Catechesis*, 6, 5 (PG 33, 545).

28 Thomas à Kempis, *The Imitation of Christ*, III, 14.

29 St Augustine, *Confessions*, VII, 10; XI, 9.

30 Cf. Otto, *op. cit.* (see note 12 above).

31 St Francis of Assisi, *Paraphrase of the 'Our Father'* in *The Words of St Francis*, ed. Meyer, Chicago, Franciscan Herald Press, 1982, p. 25.

32 St Irenaeus, *Adversus Haereses*, III, 25, 2.

33 Cf. Otto, *op. cit.* chapter 13 (see note 12 above).

34 Martin Luther, *In Psalmos* (WA 5, p. 163).

35 Roman Missal, *Collect for 26th Sunday in Ordinary Time*.

36 G. Ungaretti, *Poesie*, Milan, Mondadori, 1988, p. 72.

37 Cf. St Gregory Nazianzen, *Orationes*, 28, 3 (PG 36, 29); St Bonaventure, *Arbor Vitae* 30, ed. Cousins, N.Y., Paulist Press, 1978.

38 Luther, Hymn *'Ein feste Burg ist unser Gott'*.

39 Roman Missal, *Collect for 12th Sunday in Ordinary Time*.

40 E. Kant, *The Only Possible Ground of Proof for the Existence of God*, preface, in *Werke* 2, Berlin, 1905, p. 65; *Critique of Practical Reason*, conclusion, in *Werke* 5, Berlin, 1913, p. 161.

41 Cf. C. Péguy, *Le porche du mystère de la deuxième vertu*, in *Oeuvres poétiques*, Paris, Gallimard, 1975, pp. 531–7.

42 Dante, *Paradiso*, XXXIII, 142.

43 J. Kepler, *De Harmonice Mundi*, V, 10 in *Opera Omnia* 5, Frankfurt-Erlangen, 1864, p. 327.

44 St Augustine, *Confessions*, X, 7 & 25.

45 Ibid., *Enarrationes in Psalmos*, 130, 12 (CCL 40, p. 1907f).

46 Ibid., *In Iohannis Evangelium*, 18, 10 (CCL 36, p. 186); *De vera religione*, 39, 72 (CCL 32, p. 234).

47 A monk, *Les portes du silence*, Geneva, Librairie Claude Martingay (no date).

48 St Augustine, *Soliloquies*, I, 1, 3; II, 1, 1 (PL 32, 870 & 885).

49 Søren Kierkegaard, *The Sickness unto Death*, 2, 1, 1, OUP, 1941.

50 B. Pascal, *Pensées*, 347, ed. Brunschvig.

51 *Little Flowers of St Francis: Third Consideration on the Holy Stigmata*, (St Francis of Assisi, *Writings and Early Biographies*, Chicago, 1983, p. 1446).

52 J. H. Newman, *Apologia pro vita sua*, I & IV, 2 & 5, London, Longmans Green, 1902; *Letters and Correspondence*, p. 25.

53 Cf. Kant, *The Only Possible Ground* (see note 40 above), summary, part 3.

54 Dionysius the Areopagite, *The Mystical Theology*, I, 3 (PG 3, 1001) tr. Rolt, London, SPCK, 1951, p. 192.

55 Pascal, *op. cit.*, 267.

56 St Thomas Aquinas, *In Boethii Trinitatem Proem.*, q. 1, a. 2, ad 1, tr. Brennan, London, Herder Books, 1946, p. 31.

57 St Augustine, *Epistles*, 130, 28 (PL 33, 505).

58 Kierkegaard, *The Journals*, VIII A 11.

59 St John of the Cross, *The Dark Night: Stanzas of the Soul*, 3–4.

60 *The Book of Blessed Angela of Foligno*, N.Y., Paulist Press, 1993, pp. 238–9.

61 *The Cloud of Unknowing*, 5, (see note 15 above) p. 28.

62 St Augustine, *Confessions*, IX, 10, 23–26.

63 St Anselm, *Proslogion*, 1 (see note 8 above) p. 97.

64 Jan van Ruysbroek, *Die Zierde der geistlichen Hochzeit*, 41.

65 Rabindranath Tagore, *Gitanjali*, 42.

66 Theophilus of Antioch, *Ad Autolicum*, 1, 2.

67 Pascal, *op. cit.*, 240.

68 St Basil the Great, *De Spiritu Sancto*, IX, 23 (PG 32, 109).

69 Diadochus of Photike, *Ascetic Discourses*, 58 (SCh 5bis, p. 118).

70 M. Basilea Schlink, *Wie ich Gott erlebte*, Darmstadt, 1976.

71 Nikos Kazantzakis, *God's Pauper*, Oxford, Cassirer, 1962, p. 118.

72 Dionysius the Areopagite, *The Divine Names*, II, 9 (PG 3, 648) – 'pati divina'.

73 Johannes Tauler, *Homily* 40 in *Johannes Tauler, Predigten*, ed. Hofmann, Freiburg im Breisgau, 1961, p. 305.

74 *Book of Blessed Angela* (see note 60 above), p. 313.

75 Cf. St Simeon the New Theologian, *Catechesis* XXIII & XXV–XXVI (SCh 113, pp. 112ff).

76 St Irenaeus, *op. cit.*, IV, 20, 7.

77 St Bernard, *De gradibus humilitatis*, 10, 36 (PL 182, 962).

78 Goethe, *Faust* Part II, Act V – 'Alles Vergaengliche ist nur ein Gleichnis.'

79 Sartre, *Le Diable et le Bon Dieu*, Paris, Gallimard, 1951.

80 Ludwig Andreas Feuerbach, *Das Wesen des Christentums*, 2nd ed. 1842; *Geschichte der neueren Philosophie*, 2nd ed. 1844; *Das Wesen der Religion*, 1845.

81 Karl Marx, *Luther as judge between Strauss & Feuerbach* in *Werke*, 1, Berlin, 1964, p. 27.

82 Ibid., *Critique of Hegel's Philosophy of Law* in *Gesamtausgabe* I, 1, Frankfurt am Main, 1927.

83 Sigmund Freud, *Leonardo da Vinci and a memory of his*

Childhood in _Complete Psychological Works_, vol. 11, London, Hogarth, p. 123.

84 Pope John Paul II, Encyclical: _Dominum et vivificantem_, 37.

85 Francis Bacon, _Essay_ XVI, _On Atheism_.

86 Freud, _The Future of an Illusion_ in _Complete Psychological Works_ (see note 83 above) vol. 21, p. 33.

87 Origen, _Contra Celsum_, V, 1 (SCh 147, p. 16), tr. Chadwick, CUP, 1980, p. 264 (adapted).

88 St Augustine, _Enarrationes in Psalmos_, 93, 15 (CCL 39, p. 1316).

89 Feuerbach in _Saemtliche Werke_, 7, p. 2.

90 Kierkegaard, _The Sickness unto Death_, I, C (see note 49 above).

91 Cf. Tertullian, _Apologeticum_, 24, 10 – '_Deus cuius, velimus ac nolimus, omnes sumus_'; St Augustine, _Soliloquies_, I, 1, 2 – '_Deus, quem amat omne quod potest amare, sive sciens sive nesciens_'; Prayer over the Offerings for Saturday in the 4th week of Lent – '_ad te nostras etiam rebelles compelle propitius voluntates_'.

92 F. Nietzsche, _The Joyful Wisdom_ in _Complete Works_, Somerset UK, Foulis, 1899–1915.

93 P. Claudel, _Cinq grands odes_, III, in _Oeuvre poétique_, Paris, Gallimard, 1967, p. 251.

94 M. Blondel in _Vocabulaire technique et critique de la philosophie_, ed. Lalande, 7th edition, Paris, 1956, p. 229f.

95 Tertullian, _Adversus Marcionem_, II, 27 (CCL 1, p. 506).

96 Kant, _The Only Possible Ground_ (see note 40 above).

97 G.W.F. Hegel, _Fruehe Schriften_, 1 (text 34) in _Gesammelte Werke_, I, Hamburg, 1989, p. 372.

98 Erik Fromm, _You shall be as Gods_, tr. Holt, N.Y., Rinehart & Winston, 1966, chapter 2.

99 Tertullian, _Adversus Marcionem_, II, 16 (CCL 1, p. 492).

100 Sartre, _Le Diable et le Bon Dieu_ (see note 79 above) section X.

101 Tertullian, _Adversus Marcionem_, II, 27, 6 (CCL 1, p. 506).

102 G. Lessing, _Eine Duplik_ 1, in _Werke_ 3, Zurich, 1974, p. 149.

103 F. Dostoevsky, _Notes from Underground_, 9.

104   Kierkegaard, *Journals*, VII A 181.

105   St Gregory Nazianzen, *Carmina*, 29 (PG 37, 507).

106   Cf. St Athanasius, *Contra Arianos*, I, 18 (PG 26, 49).

107   Eusebius of Caesarea, *Ecclesiastical History*, V, 28, 5.

108   Evagrius, *De oratione*, 61 (PG 79, 1165).

109   Cf. A. Solignac, *Théologie* in *Dictionnaire de Spiritualité* XV, 1990, cols. 463–87.

110   E. Iserloh, in *Handbuch der Kirchengeschichte*, V, 2, Das Spätmittelalter, Ed. H. Jedin, Freiburg im Br., 1968, ch. 41.

111   Kierkegaard, *The Sickness unto Death* (see note 49 above), preface.

112   Diadochus of Photike, *One hundred Chapters*, 7 (SCh 5bis, p. 87).

113   St Thomas Aquinas, *Opuscula theologica*, ed Marietti, vol. 2, p. 285.

114   Id., *Summa Theologiae* I–IIae, q. 106, 2.

115   Tommaso de Vio (Cajetanus), *Commentary on the Summa Theologiae of St Thomas, In Primam*, q. 63, a. 3, 13 – '. . . *dum superbe vellemus in nostris quiescere, divina Deo relinquendo.*'

116   Goethe, *Menschengefuehl* in *Gedichte*, Stuttgart, Reclam, 1992, p. 73.

117   *Imitation of Christ*, III, 2.

118   Origen, *Commentary on St Luke's Gospel*, fragment 18 (GCS 49, p. 227).

119   St Gregory of Nyssa, *De eo qui sit ad imaginem Dei*, (PG 44, 1340).

120   H. Muehlen, in *The Spirit and the Church*, ed. Martin, N.Y., 1976, pp. 177ff.

121   St Basil the Gt., *De Spiritu Sancto*, 19, 49 (PG 32, 157).

122   Giacomo Leopardi, *L'Infinito*.

123   Cf. Dionysius the Areopagite, *The Mystical Theology*, III (PG 3, 1033) (see note 54 above).

124   Nietzsche, *The Joyful Wisdom*, nr. 135 (see note 92 above).

125   Kierkegaard, *Christian Discourses & the Lilies of the Field*, tr. Lowrie, 1939.

126 Péguy, *Le mystère des Saints Innocents* in *Oeuvres poétiques* (see note 41 above), p. 692.

127 Cf. Kierkegaard, *Journals*, XI² A 154.

128 Cf. St Augustine, *Enarrationes in Psalmos* 85, 1 (CCL 39, p. 1176).

129 St Basil the Gt., *De Spiritu Sancto* 26, 62 (PG 32, 181ff).

130 *The Spirit and the Church* (see note 120 above), p. 16.

131 Roman Missal, *Common Preface*, IV.

132 Gregory of Tours, *History of the Franks*, II, 31 (PL 71, 227).

133 G. Tersteegen, *Geistliches Blumengaertlein*, 11, Stuttgart, 1969, p. 340f.

134 Tagore, *Gitanjali*, 38.

135 Cf. M. Horkheimer, *Die Sehnsucht nach dem ganz Anderen*, Hamburg, 1970.

136 St Augustine, *In Iohannis Evangelium* 40, 10; *In Epistolus Iohannis* 4, 6; *Enarrationes in Psalmos* 37, 14; *Epistola* 130, 10, 20.

137 Roman Missal, *Collect for Tuesday in the 1st week of Lent – 'desiderio tui fulgeat.'*

138 *The Cloud of Unknowing* 4 & 6 (see note 15 above) pp. 27 & 29.

139 Isaac of Nineveh, *Ascetic Discourses*, 4, Rome, Città Nuova, 1984, p. 89.

140 Cf. Archimandrite Sophrony, *op. cit.* (see note 2 above).

141 St Ignatius of Antioch, *Letter to the Romans*, 7, 2.

142 St Bonaventure, *Itinerarium mentis in Deum*, 7, 4.

143 St Augustine, *Confessions*, X, 27.

144 Angelus Silesius, *op. cit.* VI, 263 (see note 3 above).

145 Cf. John & Charles Wesley, *Selected Writings & Hymns*, ed. Whaling, N.Y., Paulist Press, 1981, p. 387.

146 St Augustine, *Confessions*, III, 6.